No Feet In Concrete
Leadership In An Entrepreneurial World

John F. Boogaert

First Edition

A

PANAGRAPH

Publication

**Publisher's Cataloging-in-Publication
(Provided by Quality Books, Inc.)**

Boogaert, John F.
    No feet in concrete : leadership in an entrepreneurial world / John F.
    Boogaert -- 1st ed.
    p. cm.
    LCCN: 00-103862
    ISBN: 0-9700981-5-4
    1. Leadership. 2. Business planning. 3. Entrepreneurship.
    4. Management. I. Title.

HD57.7.B66 2000   658.4'092
                   QBI00-533

Published by:
Panagraph, Inc.
www.panagraph.com

For my wife, Brooke and our daughters,
Allison and Melissa.

TABLE OF CONTENTS

Acknowledgements

Introduction

ACKNOWLEDGEMENTS

It is a great pleasure to acknowledge the many people who have contributed to the process of creating this book.

Dewey Johnson, Professor of Management at the Sid Craig School of Business, California State University, Fresno, provided invaluable needling and encouragement from the very beginning of the project. Special thanks, Dewey.

Recognition is more than due to the participants of the *No Feet In Concrete* seminars who took the time to tell us how they used this new process to create an effective and unique leadership style. Special credit is certainly due to all the strong leaders who I've had the pleasure to work with for so many years. Observing your effective leadership has formed the spirit of this book.

To all the insightful people at Panagraph who added their measure of quality and spirit to this book, a sincere note of appreciation. Special thanks to Ross Yukawa for the cover, Sheri Bohigian for putting the copy to the test, Christine Sherburne for the interior layout and design, and Mike Fitzgerald for his keen insight at just the right times.

We sincerely appreciated the input from Mike Villines, Bill Patnaude, Michele Cantwell-Copher and others who took the time to read *No Feet In Concrete* before it went to press. No doubt, your input made this book a better read.

I am especially pleased to acknowledge the support of Panagraph's Board of Directors, Mike Villines, Mark Astone, Vern Crow and Brooke Blakely Boogaert who encouraged me to carve out the time to write this book. Specific thanks to

Directors Steve Farris and Paula Neale Farris whose original commitment and insight has been a powerful element in the formation and continuing development of Panagraph.

This book would not have been possible without the commitment and special contributions from Stella Bohigian, the *No Feet In Concrete* Program Director, who gave more hours to the success of this project than I would want to know about. Her dedication to both concept and detail is a vital part of this book. Thank you, Stella, for helping me to simplify and focus. Your ongoing support is deeply appreciated.

Finally, I would like to acknowledge the continual insight, support and encouragement from my wife, Brooke Blakely Boogaert. Her ongoing input on the manuscript was invaluable. From her early days as Panagraph's first sound engineer to her current role as Chief Financial Officer, her quiet, powerful contribution has been an essential component in both Panagraph's success and my own personal sense of satisfaction and professional achievement. Thank you, Brooke.

Thank you all; this has been a wonderful project!

INTRODUCTION

Leadership is challenging in any venue. In many businesses, at home, in volunteer organizations or in schools, government offices or military operations, the entrepreneurial approach is quickly becoming the strategy of choice. While entrepreneurial energy can provide strong direction and power, how does it translate into an effective leadership style? Unfortunately, in a world of continual change, many styles of conventional management are doomed to fail.

> How can you ensure that you will be able to develop a leadership style to take advantage of the spontaneous opportunities hiding in an entrepreneurial world of perpetual change? How can you make certain that your leadership approach will produce spectacular results?

The response to this opportunity is the foundation of this book. It is a guide for *you* to build your own leadership style that will drive *your* operation – with your skills, your values, your objectives and, most of all, the people in your organization – at *this* time in history.

If you've been frustrated reading about how other leaders crafted leadership styles that worked well for their companies, but you intuitively sense will not work for you, there **is** light at the end of the tunnel.

No Feet In Concrete will guide and support your efforts as you begin to develop your own unique leadership style . . . one that will work for you and others in your operation.

CHAPTER 1

The Search for a
Real Leadership Strategy

*"I've read dozens of books on management
theory. The ideas all sound good when
you're reading them, but they just don't
seem to fit what we are doing or the people
in our organization. I've used a few ideas
but I just can't seem to find a style that
lights a long-term fire. No more false starts,
no more 'feel good' meetings with no results
– we need to get focused and operate at a
totally different speed."*

- Looking at the Alternatives

- Rethink, Don't Imitate

- So What's Wrong With Tom Peters?

- Entrepreneurial Leadership

- The Challenge

- Maps for Success

Looking at the Alternatives

If you are seriously looking for a resource that will light a fire in your organization, you are not alone. A quick click on Amazon.com lists thousands of books on "Management", and even a short stop at an airport bookstand will give you more titles than you could digest in six months of concentrated effort. If Management is really a science, as so many have suggested over the years, why would we need thousands of different books with thousands of different theories? There seem to be as many resources out there as there are wildly successful ventures. Confusing to be sure.

In his recent book, **Management Challenges in the 21st Century,** Peter Drucker expanded on the popular theory that we should *manage **things*** (inventory, equipment, cash flow, etc.) but *lead **people.*** While the concept seems to oppose the title of his book, the point is well taken. Given the nature of the contemporary workplace, the concept of managing stuff and leading people is a profound key to great 21st century leadership. Management can no longer be seen as manipulation. Today's high-performing GenXers don't need, nor will they tolerate, manipulation. However, they do demand the finest leadership skills that we can generate. As you move forward toward extracting a powerful leadership style for your organization, it is time to abandon the concept of "Management" and move solidly toward a style of "Leadership" that will, in fact, free up the power within your organization for dramatic movement, growth and success.

Rethink, Don't Imitate

In 1997, I knew that our own company, Panagraph, Inc. was on the verge of dramatic growth. We had recruited a new group of highly-skilled, ambitious GenX leaders who were acutely focused on success. I read everything I could get my hands on to see if I could find a style to guide us to the results that I knew were possible. Fortunately for us all, our new recruits would not accept the same old tired leadership styles that they had read about as they were getting their BAs and MBAs. Even our seasoned employees had become impatient as we tried to blend so many unique personal styles into a focused leadership pattern.

While readings, tapes, articles and lectures challenged us to rethink how we were doing things, we were left short at a critical juncture. There was simply no material available to help us develop a unique leadership style that fit our company, with our range of experience, our talents and our unique opportunities for dramatic growth.

The value of looking at other styles was that we were definitely rethinking how to lead our own company. Unfortunately, our good intentions were continually frustrated because we were attempting to apply conventional management models to our company's unique opportunity.

When we look at successful ventures and systematically attempt to extract leadership theories from them, the result can be as varied as the difference between William Ouchi's *Theory Z,* and Ken Blanchard's *One Minute Manager.* Consider the mental stretch between Edward Deming's "quality control circles" and Tom Peters' *Crazy Times Call for Crazy Organizations.* You can be sure that the solution is not simply to look for Regis McKenna's most recent release on how to run a contemporary operation.

Many years ago, I got a call from a medical administrator who had just engaged in a very enthusiastic conversation with a top physician in his medical group. Their discussion focused on Tom Peters' classic, *In Search of Excellence.* He asked how I could help his group of doctors put this strategy to work to improve customer satisfaction and increase bottom line profit? Having recently read the book and being ready for a new challenge, I gladly accepted what rapidly became a frustrating experience. The book was popular at the time, the physicians and their administrator seemed ready for growth, and I had some experience consulting in the medical environment – it looked like a slam dunk, win – win.

The result will be mercifully limited to a single paragraph. The physicians found that there was a fatal disconnect between the companies that were chronicled in Peters' book and their own personal styles and schedules. My big challenge quickly turned to finding an efficient way to overlap these industrial management models with this specific medical operation and these particular physicians. Peters' book had raised expectations, but offered no clear connection between theory and practice. After more than two months of struggling with Peters' book, we concluded that while it had raised some valuable questions, it had become a boat anchor as we tried to make their medical practice look and feel like a combination of Boeing, McDonalds, Xerox and 3M.

In the final analysis these doctors didn't want to search for ways that other leaders had achieved excellence in their companies, they wanted to develop success in their own enterprise and make it produce bottom line results.

So What's Wrong With Tom Peters?

What's wrong with "searching for excellence?" At times, we all attempt to pattern our success after the success of others. Unfortunately, in an entrepreneurial world, looking for a management style by trying to recreate the success of others just doesn't seem to work. Studying successful management theories that have driven other companies simply doesn't make us effective leaders. We read about the latest and greatest companies and then spend months trying to mold our firms to look like them. The underlying assumption is that their management style will work for us as well as it did for them. Unfortunately, as we have all discovered, somehow it doesn't.

We've all read Tom Peters' books. Many of us have heard him speak. Let's face it – it's just flat fun to listen to Tom Peters. He strikes at the heart of things because he knows what we struggle with day to day – attempting to lead people and manage stuff. And, Tom Peters has watched success. From Hewlett Packard to Cisco Systems, Silicon Valley has exploded beyond the sleepy days that characterized the times when I grew up in Palo Alto. Today's *anything.com* is tomorrow's hot IPO. So what's wrong with Tom Peters' chronicles of success and lectures that consistently cause us to rethink how we lead organizations?

A couple of years ago Tom Peters spoke in San Francisco at The Commonwealth Club of California. Amusing and provocative as usual, his ideas drew a host of great questions from the full house. At the end of the hour the moderator asked "the last question", which is designed to give the speaker an opportunity to send the crowd off with a smile.

"Mr. Peters, your words today were both insightful and well received. Our final question may be coming from someone with a hidden motive, but I'll read it as it is written, 'What companies are you watching at this time?'" Tom saw the whole picture immediately and responded, "If you are looking for some inside information that will bring you future financial success, watch my real estate investments. I have the unique ability to **pick them at the very peak of their value.**" The result: a huge laugh and thunderous applause – the perfect finale from the consummate presenter.

A week later, I received the newsletter published by The Commonwealth Club of California that included a printed transcript of the week's most notable speech. There was Peters' speech right down to the final question – a near word perfect rendition of an hour with Tom Peters at his best with one notable mistake. His answer to the final question **read** as follows. "If you are interested in some inside information that will bring you sure financial success, **watch my real estate investments.**"

Big Difference!

Tom's humorous comment about picking real estate "at the peak of its value" had been reduced to just "watching his real estate investments."

Similar to his investments in real estate, Peters' chronicles of successful companies were highly focused snapshots of their operations at the "very peak of their value." **In Search of Excellence** revealed how industry giants were organized and how these outstanding company leaders operated their ventures while producing dramatic results. But Peters' highlights of these great companies do not address the real task at hand for leaders operating today in an entrepreneurial world.

The unique qualities of specific organizations do not allow us to simply import a singular strategy, no matter how well it may have worked for another organization. The real question is not *what* the leader of each organization was doing at the peak of their success but (1) *how* they developed such a unique leadership process for their specific circumstances and (2) *how* they recruited, inspired and reoriented their staff to operate in these unique ways?

Powerful, well-known companies chronicled in books on management tactics are often the acknowledged giants of industrial success. However, studying their operations and attempting to utilize their management styles is like trying to ride a bicycle looking backward. Before any organization begins a truly successful venture, the required analysis, problem solving and planning must be done, even if it is entirely intuitive. This all takes considerable time after the appointed leader recognizes the opportunity presented by a leadership change. Limiting our alternatives to these corporate snapshots, we are reduced to looking backward through many years of reading, publishing, book writing, recognition, success, labor, assessment, experience and struggle. Our fruitless exercise becomes the application of a strategy that is years old and bears little resemblance to our opportunities, staff, corporate culture and accepted objectives . . . a certain recipe for failure.

Entrepreneurial Leadership

The real answer is clearly embedded in this all too common experience. We are not interested in what other successful leaders do to run their companies. We are interested in:

- ♦ How these leaders concluded that they needed to develop a unique way to lead their ventures.

- ♦ How these gifted people developed their unique strategies.

- ♦ How they got their entire operation to want to make real changes in the way they worked together.

♦ How they inspired people to stay focused on strategic goals and not get their feet stuck in concrete.

Addressing these essential, process-oriented concepts will allow you to confidently move forward toward the development of a unique strategy for leading your operations.

You *are* operating in an entrepreneurial world – moving at a pace that you probably thought impossible just a year ago. Normal time expectations have been literally cut in half. All of our productivity tools have simply helped us to do more work in less time. We are all beginning to work on "e-time," as one of our clients so often says.

Whether you are an experienced executive in a fast-moving startup or the leader of a new product line ready to lock-on to a new opportunity; the principal of a school or the director of a non-profit; a government leader looking for ways to improve the services your staff provides or an athletic coach with a team of strong individuals, the first move is to abandon the lure of imitating other leaders' successes and tap into the strengths that are hiding within you and your current staff.

The Challenge

The challenge is to apply your own entrepreneurial skills to the actual creation of a strong, consistent leadership strategy that will:

♦ Lead your staff's feet out of concrete

♦ Lead the people to whom you report out of concrete

♦ Add energy to your operation

♦ Provide internal direction to your staff's decision-making

♦ Channel useful feedback into productive change

♦ Allow you to take advantage of instant opportunities

♦ Help you recruit and retain the most talented people available

♦ Utilize integrity as the internal driver

♦ Inspire others to make radical goals become reality

♦ Employ Entrepreneurial Leadership, not micro-management or micro-manipulation

Maps for Success

Panagraph's first film project, which was shot in 1977, took the entire company to East Germany and Poland. It was a documentary on the life of Dietrich Bonhoeffer, a well-known German theologian who, with relatives, planned several unsuccessful attempts on Hitler's life during World War II. At that time, while the East German socialist government supported the film project because Bonhoeffer was an anti-fascist, the Berlin Wall was a frightening reality.

The East German government provided Panagraph with a professional "guide" named Hans. Hans turned out to be a highly educated, fascinating person who had spent a good deal of time in the United States. After a few weeks, Hans turned to me and asked a most surprising question. He had not discussed politics with us at any time and had carefully listened for comments from our crew that would give him insight into our intentions. His question has never left me as we have appreciated our entrepreneurial enterprise and the vast opportunities for success that it has afforded us.

Hans finally asked, "Do you know what we envy most about those of you who live in the West?" He waited patiently for an answer as I wondered exactly what to say.

Put yourself in my position for a moment and dive into the question – what would you have said?

"Freedom?" I responded.

"Not close," he replied.

"Books?" (The largest bookstore in East Germany was no larger than an average Starbucks.)

"Wrong again," he said, obviously waiting for another response.

"Higher pay for professional jobs?" I was obviously reaching here, but a specific answer was written indelibly in his mind.

His answer surprised us all. "Failure – the opportunity to fail! Without it there is no opportunity to really succeed. You and those who work for your new company are clearly aware that you could fail and that very awareness means that you have a clear image of success and how to get there. Here in East

Germany our government prevents failure and, as it does, it also depresses success. Mediocrity is the norm. You and your company have the opportunity to fail, but hiding in that possibility is the map to certain success. Here in East Germany we have neither."

Truly, in so many western-developed countries, most of us have the opportunity for both failure *and* the keys to success. That specific reality often lights an entrepreneurial fire that can drive legendary leadership and success in every corner of the world where free enterprise is an alternative.

As entrepreneurs, we dream of success and how to make it happen in new and different ways. As entrepreneurs, we expect results that others often see as irrational. We see opportunity and success where others see closed doors and failure. As entrepreneurs who are keenly aware of the paths to failure, we see a map to success where others simply see chaos.

Most entrepreneurs apply innovative ideas and drivers to the new products and services they develop, as well as to their operations, distribution and sales. Unfortunately, those same entrepreneurs rarely utilize their vision to move beyond the one big obstacle that so often spells certain limitation and failure for any entrepreneurial enterprise.

The big "cement shoes" for the entrepreneurial enterprise is *micro-management,* which will block vital arteries at the very heart of corporate operations and culture. The problem that so many entrepreneurs face is that nearly all contemporary leadership theories are, in actuality, simply ways to redirect, motivate and control the people you are really trying to lead. Micro-management is really micro-manipulation. If your work is centered upon redirection, motivation and control, you can be sure that you will never be in a position to become a true leader in an entrepreneurial world.

To be sure, *No Feet In Concrete* leadership is not the next generation of micro-manipulation. *No Feet In Concrete* is a strategic tool to ensure that you will break free of old management styles and, at the same time, utilize powerful, entrepreneurial principles to develop a distinctive leadership method that will lead your operation to the results that only you can imagine.

Summing It Up

First we looked at the ways that we have all tried to make management styles fit our specific organizations. Management theories are more diverse than the corporate cultures that drive our efforts. Other styles just don't seem to fit our unique operations. Likewise, imposing the latest management strategies can lead to genuine frustration, stagnation and unnecessary failure.

While examining other theoretical management methods affords us the opportunity to rethink exactly how we lead entrepreneurial ventures, applying those tactics can put our feet in concrete by encouraging us to imitate styles that were never intended for our operations.

Next we discovered the questions that we are really interested in. *How* did those dynamic leaders get to the point where they were operating with a radically new and effective leadership and operational style that worked for their specific operations? It is the *Hows* not the *Whats* that are the keys to successful leadership.

One real key to success hides in the very opportunity to fail. This concept is often seen by the true leader but rarely seen by operational managers. Fearing failure, these managers miss the potent map and deep motivation hiding within the opportunity to fail.

Finally, we pointed to what you can expect from this book and how it will help you use *your* entrepreneurial skills to avoid micro-management and create a dynamic strategy that will drive your staff to dramatic goals.

Questions and Actions

Here are some questions that will begin to help you apply your entrepreneurial skills to the development of your unique leadership style. They can make great conversation. We use them at our seminars, and we'll begin the next chapter with some of the ideas that have been brought up here for discussion and thought. Enjoy.

1. Make a list of all the Management styles you have been exposed to, or been a victim of, in your career to date. You may enjoy actually writing them down in the column for future reference and amusement.

2. Think specifically about where your organization's feet are in concrete. (Not people but organizational assumptions, habits and processes.) Don't lose the faith here – we're going to get those important feet *out* of the cement! We always have a good time with this at the seminars. If you're not laughing a bit here, quickly raise your feet a few critical inches and move on to the next question.

3. Which books have been most helpful? Any ideas that have worked to date with your leadership/management staff? You might want to be sure that you are wearing your thickest skin here. Are there any useful insights that you would want to consider as you begin to develop your own personal leadership style?

4. How did a heightened awareness of failure drive your most
   prized personal success? This hidden map is the real heart of
   entrepreneurial leadership.

CHAPTER 2
Carving Assets

"Our product manager has absolutely no idea what I do on a day-to-day basis. We set up some goals and objectives that fit with what he wanted to accomplish, but he never asked me what I thought we should be doing or how to do it. Sure, he trusts me to get the job done, but he is only interested in meeting his goals and objectives. Frankly, he knows so little about me or my contribution to the process, I'm constantly surprised that we do as well as we do. We could accomplish so much more."

- Your List
- Popular Responses
- Carving a Seal
- The True *No Feet in Concrete* Key
- Carving and Leadership
- The Real Basics

Your List

We would love to know what made your hit list of useless "management" methods. Some of our favorites, which have been cited at seminars, are as follows:

- ♦ Management by Objectives
- ♦ One-Minute Management
- ♦ MBWA
- ♦ Quality Control Circles
- ♦ Theory Z
- ♦ Psycho-Theories from the 1960s
- ♦ Zen and the Art of Business Management
- ♦ Management Induced Chaos
- ♦ Lessons from Dictators
- ♦ Ping-Up Management
- ♦ The time-honored classic: Y.S.T.
  (Yell, Scream and Threat)

No doubt you've had some experience with *Management by Objectives* in one form or another. How long did it take you to learn to express your objectives in a way that would ensure that you could achieve them? How long did it take to figure out that many of your managers really didn't care if you achieved your objectives as long as they reached theirs? How often did anyone really look at your objectives? If your answer is "once per year," like most of our seminar participants, you can be sure that your objectives didn't do much to enhance your value to or coordinate your work with the overall endeavor – until a week before you had your performance review.

A close second in popularity to *Management by Objectives* has been a variety of clever additions to standard management activities such as MBWA (Management by Walking Around) or Ken Blanchard's *The One Minute Manager.*

In addition there are a host of textbooks that offer management and leadership analysis – both historical and contemporary. However, most of these references become more of a rite of passage for the new generation of business students than useful resources to develop functional models for leading people in an entrepreneurial world.

As humorous as this exercise can be and as varied as the responses have been, this exercise quickly points to four salient observations:

- ◆ There is a broadly perceived need to understand how to lead people.

- ◆ There are no standard management strategies that have delivered broadly applied, long-term results.

- ◆ Effective leaders seem to finally discard all standardized strategies and create new paradigms for their own unique circumstances.

- ◆ Leaders are more prone to write about how they ended up leading their organizations than how they developed their own particular approach to leadership.

Popular Responses

We always enjoy this discussion about management styles at our seminars because it reliably brings out some very tired or long forgotten management theories and a lot of laughs. Why the laughing? It is more than obvious that these imported theories have been ineffective at least and amusing at best.

Most of these popular strategies have been grounded in what was an intrinsically flawed task, doomed by its very assumptions. Each of these strategies involve methods designed to get others to do something that they were unmotivated, unwilling or unable to do by relying on their own internal motivations. Somehow these management concepts were designed to get people "in line" and keep them there. The clear assumption was that if you didn't "manage" them, they would quickly wander off into unproductive chaos. When these folks got their job done, we had managed them well. When they failed we had managed them poorly. What a bizarre assumption.

Underlying this flawed concept is the assumption that "management" is the fundamental key to operational success. As we all know so well from being victims of these kinds of assumptions, they are simply not true. Once again, we see micro-manipulation rearing its ugly head at the very root of management theories.

Carving a Seal

While studying film theory and production at Claremont I was drawn to the work of Robert Flaherty, the true artistic pioneer of documentary film. Now years later, Flaherty's method for creating documentary film has become a fundamental element in our process of catalyzing the development and installation of customized leadership strategies.

Robert Flaherty's earliest work was titled "Nanook of the North," a documentary film about a family of Arctic Native Americans who survived within what seemed to be an impossible world. This film was a true classic about a culture engaged in an annual life or death struggle against nature. In fact, Nanook and family did not survive the winter following Flaherty's experience with them.

In *The Innocent Eye,* Frances Flaherty's book on her husband's documentary process, she recounts his observation that the Eskimo people seemed to have a unique ability to carve. No doubt you have seen these graceful carvings of soapstone or ivory. Simple, expressive and full of energy, Eskimos seem to capture the essence of an animal in poses as natural as life.

Curious about this process, Flaherty asked Nanook about his apparently innate ability to carve. Nanook seemed puzzled by the question. It was as obvious to Nanook that everyone could carve as it seemed unnatural to Flaherty that these Eskimos did it so easily.

Nanook revealed that, in fact, most all Eskimos carve figures but that it really takes very little skill. They carry a piece of ivory around with them for long periods of time, whittling a bit or perhaps even chewing on it gently but always asking the same fundamental question:

"What's hiding here? What's hiding here?"

The process continues until the carver suddenly sees the figure inside the medium. A seal is seen hiding there within the ivory.

Then, Nanook explained, "The process is simple. You simply carve away what isn't seal." Note that the carver doesn't imagine a figure of a seal in his mind and then impose it upon the ivory. Quite the contrary – the question continues until the carver sees the seal within the ivory. At this point the process is ultimately simple. The carver simply "cuts away what isn't seal."

No frustration that the ivory has an internal crack or flaw. No concern that the carver cannot afford the proper size piece of ivory to compliment his vision. No frustration coming from attempting to carve a preconceived seal out of the piece of ivory at hand. And finally, spectacular results with no need for anyone to manage the work.

The carver's internal motivation and confidence in the process drives their work. The carver's mind is held to a discipline of asking, "What's hiding here?" There is never a thought of imposing a style or copying previous work. Their own special seeing into the ivory gives the work both form and function. The reward is the discovery of form and the freeing of the true and elegant seal from within the raw ivory. And finally, there is never confusion as to the reason for the

grace and brilliance of the seal – it was the seal
hiding inside not the hand or mind of the carver.
The entire process of questioning and discovery
may take months, while the actual final carving
may take minutes.

Nanook's unique response was to become the foundation for
Flaherty's original approach to documentary film and a
standard for documentary film to this day: (1) let the camera
"see" everything that moves; (2) watch the footage and look
carefully for the "seal" that is hiding there; (3) remove what
isn't profoundly relevant; and (4) arrange what you have left in
the most powerful and expressive form that reveals the
original subject.

Managers often become frustrated, losing patience with the
deeper process and rush, far too quickly, to "carve" it up. True
leaders understand the value of profoundly asking, "What's
hiding here?" They have learned four fundamental facts.

(1) All truly reliable leadership strategies begin with a
process of focused, genuine listening.

(2) Time is better spent "cutting away what isn't seal" –
freeing up innate talent rather than micro-manipulating
people to do things they fundamentally are not ready,
willing or able to do.

(3) A clear, new picture will emerge as to how to arrange
resources properly for maximum results.

(4) Stay out of the way and watch how well and how fast
things will get done.

The True *No Feet In Concrete* Key

How often have we found ourselves at the bottom of our conceptual bag of solutions, convinced that there simply are no viable ways to move forward? It is exactly at this moment that we let go of our imposing habits and reliance on past solutions. It is at this moment that we intuitively begin to open our hands and minds, asking the question, "What's hiding here?" It is at this moment that we begin to see the elegant seal hiding in what appears to be unstructured chaos. We have run all other solutions out to their logical conclusions. We have finally given the internally fitting solution a chance to begin to find its rightful and profitable place.

It is here that we begin to develop the root of true *No Feet In Concrete* leadership . . . questioning, listening and real discovery, not copying or imposing. It really is a constant process of asking ourselves, "What's hiding here?"

Is there any question in your mind as to why Arctic Native Americans continue to carve in this profound manner? This special spirit of discovery dominates their approach to each other as well. Carving brings the discipline of this special "revealing from within" to daily living.

Carving and Leadership

What follows are some questions to begin to apply this powerful approach to more practical leadership skills. Try to forget the various ways you have answered these kinds of questions in the past. You will also want to set aside the input you have had from other people. It's (always) time to take a fresh, thoughtful look at what you are doing and who is doing it. In the next chapter we will discuss the importance of "making a picture" with everyone and everything you want in the image – standing in the most productive and internally consistent spots.

For now, let's just start with a "blank sheet of paper" – no assumptions, no tired solutions, no excuses, no problem people, no stale old puzzle picture with pieces that don't fit anywhere.

Let's get an absolutely fresh image of *exactly* what assets you have available; then ask, "What's hiding here?"

- What do others really **want** to accomplish?

- What is hiding within our assets (both human and physical) that I have consistently missed?

- What new resources do we need to acquire to make big things happen?

- Am I asking people to do things that they are unable or unwilling to do without direct supervision? What do these people really want to do?

- Do I have "stars" stuck in boxes?

- Where are the best people hiding? Are they across the hall or across the country? Am I afraid of hiring these people?

- What internal capital resources have I missed? How can I make them work for what we are doing?

- Who are the "hidden boat anchors?" How and where am I able to make them stars? Am I truly awakening sleeping potential, or am I conducting rehab on the unwilling? What should I do with the unable or unwilling?

♦ Am I answering these kinds of questions with the same old answers that I *know* won't create new process and wild success?

And finally, to quote one of Panagraph's senior staff members,

♦ Am I leading this group to a new position or just executing a plan?

This final question is the real nutcracker. If we spend our day simply executing a plan (ours or anyone else's) we will never be seen as a leader even if we have the position, title and salary. However, if we continue to ask, "What's hiding here?" this simple question will intuitively guide us to the next all-important task of eliminating what is dysfunctional. When we have the right people doing the right jobs and eliminate dysfunctional activities, we will, in turn, begin to reveal dynamic new pictures for how to get things done.

As we begin to utilize this now unique process, we have moved our "feet **out** of concrete." And, as we do, we will begin to be identified as valued leaders regardless of our present position, title or salary.

Why do we wait until we are at the end of our limits of frustration to employ this powerful process? *Why not make it the core of how we attack each day,* each person on our staff, each resource we have at our disposal and each opportunity that presents itself to us?

This simple intuitive question, "What's hiding here?" grounds us deeply within reality. As this powerful question becomes a daily habit, we naturally begin to spend our time cutting away what is unnecessary to the essential person or task at hand.

Workable solutions jump off the page. They do not require mind games to employ nor do they produce mind games to avoid. Solutions are simple and elegant. They work because the people we lead are doing what they know they can and want to do well. They believe in your new picture because it is based on the entire group doing what they are ready and prepared to do – with no reliance on micro-manipulation and its inherent propensity for failure. You will gain everyone's confidence because they see that you listen carefully, promote their true skills and priorities and get barriers out of the way – *not* create new ones.

It is important to note that this is *NOT* an instinctive process. Our minds do not open themselves without some discipline. Making a continuous routine out of asking this fundamental question, "what's hiding here," will produce powerful, practical results. The single motivator within this course is the confidence that our entrepreneurial senses will, in fact, reveal a strong, flexible leadership strategy if we can just get our feet out of concrete, continue to ask the right questions, carve away the unnecessary and hold up a commanding new picture.

The Real Basics

Where should we begin to apply our radical question to ensure that we end up with a leadership style that won't include "management?" If we start with job related questions, we miss a critical element in the process. The real key is to dial into the deepest motivations and desires of our key players.

Early in the *No Feet In Concrete* seminars, we like to ask fundamental questions that help us understand the deeper motives driving our participants. Our most popular question is, "What would you like to do when you retire?" At first many people ask, "What does that have to do with getting our 'feet out of concrete' and addressing the task at hand?"

Despite their early reluctance, seminar participants quickly begin to discuss what they really would like to do. The results reveal volumes. Consider the following response from the marketing manager of a software company when asked the above question in a seminar.

"When I retire I would like to sail across the entire Pacific Ocean – **solo.** I have always enjoyed sailing and I can't imagine anything better than doing it solo. No phones, no computers, no reports, no tired salespeople and most of all – no whining customers referred to me by our sales staff."

What was the "seal" hiding in this response? Here was a marketing manager responsible for leading a substantial sales effort who wanted to sail **solo** across the Pacific Ocean! He didn't enjoy solving problems for his sales staff or communicating with customers? This was a person who clearly had the overt knowledge, skills and experience to lead the company's marketing efforts. However, it was more than obvious that the task didn't fit with his deeper self. I am pleased to say that even though his company recognized his surface skills and experience, they began to realize that he was not comfortable in his skin. He was clearly out of sync with real personal basics. The rest of the management staff realized that there wasn't going to be much left after they began to carve away what wasn't seal. Soon after the seminar, we were not surprised that this experienced, bright (and burned out) marketing manager realized that he needed to be doing something else or failure would be knocking at two doors, his and the company's . . . a win-win insight.

Consider another response to the same question, this time from a busy consultant and staff member in a mid-sized professional organization.

> "What I would really like to do is coach a Little League baseball team." The response was complete silence. Before this moment he had never expressed any interest in coaching. He had been active in athletics in the past but didn't have any Little League-aged children.
>
> The response from the President of the company was not what anyone expected. Having seen a real seal, he immediately began carving away. "Why would you wait until you retire? Why don't you go out and do it *now* – even if it takes you out of the office for a few hours each week."

Clearly, neither the President nor anyone on his staff had any idea that working with kids had been a part of their team member's thinking for many years. Now, the President was encouraging him to do it immediately! The President knew well that this valuable staff member needed something to do beside work 24/7 or he would be on a certain long-term professional downslide.

Little League was a way of getting in sync with some genuine basics. By supporting this activity, the President acknowledged that his staff member was getting the job done and knew that coaching would not detract from his overall contribution. The President's leadership indicated that he expected his staff to support the process. Now, the President was in a position to ask the same fundamental question of his entire staff's professional activities, which, in turn allowed him to carve away at what was holding them back from making real progress. Here was true leadership in action, not mindless management.

After this initial process of tuning into the personal basics of your staff, it is time to apply it to the beginning of your new leadership style. Continue by asking your staff, "What would you do if you were in charge and how would you do it?" Once you get the answers to this question your real task begins: Cutting away those things that prevent your staff from doing what they really want to do to create excellence in your organization.

It is obvious that if you follow this process to the outer edges of your organization, you will likely find some glaring holes – those things that no one in your group really wants to do. While acknowledging glaring holes can be unsettling as you see the real seals emerge, it is helpful to remember that nothing has changed except that you are now keenly aware of what would not have been done well or in a timely manner. It is imperative that you identify the real holes in the operation, rather than continue to micro-manipulate the flawed process, wasting valuable time and finally ensuring mediocrity.

At *No Feet In Concrete* seminars, we are frequently surprised at the results of the above discussions. Our surprise is not the content of what is expressed, but how rarely people who attempt to lead actually look for the real basics. Broad-based assumptions run long and deep. The result is that managers are often out of touch with the core issues that drive the inner thoughts and overt actions of the people they attempt to lead. When we know what occupies a person's deeper mind-set and when they feel us carve away unnecessary tasks and activities, we begin to tap into the energy of creative, authentic, entrepreneurial leadership.

Summing it up

We started this chapter making a list of the management strategies that have been a part of your experience. We have all been victims of management models that managers have, in good faith, applied to our work. We do learn from studying established theories and practices. However, importing a previously created, specific system will not inspire your staff nor will it produce an effective approach to leadership in an entrepreneurial environment. If our task is to lead others to a new position and not just manage a plan, we need a unique process – one that will work for *our* organization and *our* people at *this* time in history.

Reviewing these older, passing and trendy management methods can be a good start with your staff. A lightweight discussion about "tried and tired" methods indicates your readiness to get your feet out of concrete and will challenge others to do the same. A good, honest discussion about *Management By Objectives* techniques will also reflect your understanding that we all know how to cook the process. Your early task is to convince everyone that you are not looking for the "**S**ame **O**ld **S**tuff."

*We have made pointed use of a good-sized red SOS rubber stamp in our office. It is used on the rare occasions when staff members are seen with their feet are in concrete and are proposing the "**S**ame **O**ld **S**tuff" solutions to compelling problems. We strongly encourage you to get a customized SOS stamp for your office and have a bit of fun with it.*

Do we spend the time to discover the real assets in our organizations? Do we avoid the boat anchors inherent in reaffirming our old assumptions? Do we take the time to cut away what isn't seal or do we rely on old, shop worn impressions of our staff and how to "motivate" them? Do we look at real basics? The closer we get to understanding the core feelings and needs of our staff, the faster they will accept us as a real leader.

As you begin to carve away barriers, instead of micro-manipulating work, your team members will also quickly develop confidence that you will be the person to help them move into the right place in the new process and picture . . . the right picture – right for them and right for the entire enterprise.

Your emphasis on discovery is the first step in creating a solid, new picture, grounded in real basics, using your new, customized leadership process. The foundation will be built upon the fundamentals that you have found within your staff, the unique assets that you have discovered and the specific outside opportunities that will make success happen for you.

Questions and Actions

What follows are some activities that will help you begin to carve your assets.

1. Take a few minutes and have coffee with someone in your office. Ask them the fundamental question, "What would you like to do when you retire?" What is hiding in their response? Your further questioning should lead you to what is really behind the activities they identify.

2. Repeat the question in the context of work, "If you ran the place, what would you like to do and how would you do it?"

3. Start carving by asking, "What's holding you back from doing it NOW?" Don't allow the answer to become a list of excuses – stay practical and focused upon what the person is internally motivated to accomplish. Be sure to keep this part of the discussion in a positive mode.

4. Determine two things that you can do (within the next day or two) to help carve away at what is preventing this person from achieving real personal success. Write a note and tell the person what two things you are going to do and when you will get them done.

5. Do them both! When you have accomplished both tasks, be sure that the person knows that they have been done – on schedule.

6. Did you automatically think about doing this exercise with someone that you are currently expected to lead? Did we catch you here? This process works just as well with someone who is expected to lead **you.** Give it a try! They will instantly see you as an effective leader – taking initiative in an entrepreneurial world! *Looking for a promotion or a raise?*

7. This exercise will work unusually well with your family. If you are working with children, or have children that live with you, try the process on them. What's "hiding there?" A hidden skill? A desire to perform? A personal challenge? Commit to carving away a few things (on a specific, short timeline) that are holding them back. Be sure to let them know what you are doing. I can guarantee that you will have a wonderful experience. Both of our children have an unusual sense of self-motivation and leadership – "Eskimo carving" has served our family well for years, and now we're beginning to see our girls use the process on us!

CHAPTER 3
Making the Picture

"Our team leader makes a point of controlling our department by utilizing 'mushroom' leadership – keeping us all in the dark and feeding us 'fertilizer' if you know what I mean. He thinks that the less we know the better – that way, he thinks he is in control. The truth is that he is just managing semi-organized, unproductive chaos and doesn't know it."

- Making the Picture
- "Org" Charts Aren't Pictures
- Authority Won't Create Leadership
- Leadership Not Consensus-ship
- The New Picture
- Useful Charts
- Getters, Doers and Leaders
- Expanding the Picture

Making the Picture

The next vital step in developing your leadership strategy is to begin to make a new picture that will let your staff know where they fit in the big process and how they will relate to others on your team. In an entrepreneurial environment, simply delegating authority and demanding accountability will not work.

It is more than likely that you will help your staff look at their relationships with others in a totally different light. Most certainly they will recognize examples of leadership throughout the organization, not just in your office. This can be both frustrating and disorienting if you don't offer your staff a clear new picture of how you expect things to work.

Your new picture will now take advantage of your carving skills and a clearer understanding of the deepest potential of each person you look to lead. It is here that you reveal your new understanding of the opportunities and strengths of your operation. When you finally begin to communicate the new picture to your team, they will readily accept it because they will appreciate your genuine new insight. When they see themselves in a place where they are able to perform well, they will also realize that you have put others into areas where they will succeed, as well. Confidence in your leadership process will grow rapidly and you will be able to set far bigger goals for your group.

"Org" Charts Aren't Pictures

We have all utilized organizational charts in some manner or another. They usually involved groups of boxes arranged to indicate something about how an entire operation was organized. You can easily recall the old org charts that had one box (the big decision-maker) at the top followed by a spread of boxes that designated who reported to whom. It was understood that the boxes below did what the boxes above told them to do. This was what authority was all about – you took orders from the box above you and you gave orders to those below.

Following is an example of one of those classic Org charts.

ORGANIZATIONAL CHART

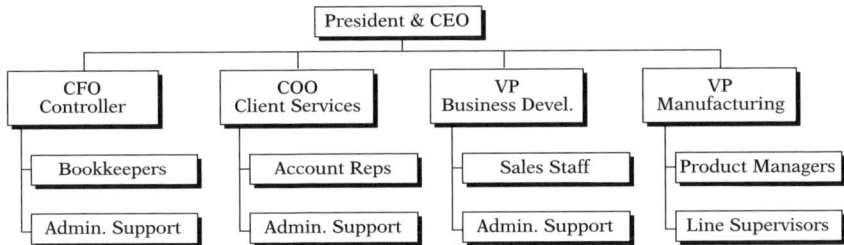

```
                        ┌──────────────────┐
                        │ President & CEO   │
                        └──────────────────┘
         ┌──────────────┬───────────────┬─────────────────┐
   ┌───────────┐  ┌───────────────┐ ┌───────────────┐ ┌───────────────┐
   │    CFO    │  │      COO      │ │      VP       │ │      VP       │
   │ Controller│  │Client Services│ │Business Devel.│ │ Manufacturing │
   └───────────┘  └───────────────┘ └───────────────┘ └───────────────┘
   ┌───────────┐  ┌───────────────┐ ┌───────────────┐ ┌────────────────┐
   │Bookkeepers│  │ Account Reps  │ │  Sales Staff  │ │Product Managers│
   └───────────┘  └───────────────┘ └───────────────┘ └────────────────┘
   ┌───────────┐  ┌───────────────┐ ┌───────────────┐ ┌────────────────┐
   │Admin.Supp.│  │ Admin. Support│ │ Admin. Support│ │Line Supervisors│
   └───────────┘  └───────────────┘ └───────────────┘ └────────────────┘
```

As an interesting observation – in these types of charts it appeared that the majority of people (at the bottom) made no decisions and had no one who was responsible to them. Organizational charts are a sure symbol of management by authority and have very little to do with identifying where real leadership exists.

During the 1960s, innovation hit org charts. We began to see circles instead of squares . . . a real sign of the times. Unfortunately, nothing else substantially changed. Managers began to talk about the importance of feedback. And when we were at the end of our ability to try to manage people, we acknowledged that those at the bottom of the chart did, on rare occasion, have something useful to add to the way managers had organized the process. Even with the advent of circles, organizational charts were still simply statements that reinforced the predominance of authority in management systems, rather than true leadership.

The next revolutionary pictures of the structure of organizations boldly put the customer at the top of the chart. After all, it was the *customer* who made the most important and final decisions. This new concept was gratuitous at best – since the president or overall leader was still seen as the self-appointed final judge interpreting and valuing the customers' input and influence in the overall decision-making process.

Authority Won't Create Leadership

A major assumption hidden in authority-based organizations is that if there is anyone below you in the organizational chart, you are able to perform as their leader. Promotions to higher levels are based on displayed task-based competence at your current level. If you are the outstanding performer at one level, it is assumed that this is an indication that you are the best candidate for the next level up the chart. And finally, if you are given additional authority, it is assumed that you know how to lead in the new position.

> Many of the dysfunctional, authority-based management actions that I have observed (and been called on to help repair) have centered on inappropriate promotions – mistaking authority for leadership. One of my most salient examples of this was a company that had lost a Vice President of marketing and sales. Heavily committed to a period of critical growth, the

company looked within its sales organization of Independent Representatives for a replacement for the Vice President. The quick choice seemed obvious – a sales person who had been setting records year after year.

Flattered by the offer, the Independent Rep took the VP position and moved his family to California. Less than two months elapsed before I received a call from the new Vice President. He said he was having trouble gaining the confidence of the other sales representatives. Could I help? A few days later I received a second call from the President of the company. He told me that he was having trouble getting the new Vice President's attention – he just didn't seem to be a team player.

Here was a perfect example of a person who was successful as an Independent Representative, operating his own small company of three people. He related well to customers and knew the various products he was selling. He was committed to the sales process and the success of his own company.

Regardless of his success as an Independent Sales Representative, he was not a specialist at relating to peers, creating an effective leadership strategy to articulate corporate goals, communicating his daily activities to a corporate President or inspiring a large group of offsite independent sales representatives.

As a field Representative, he had observed what the earlier Vice Presidents of Marketing and Sales had done right and what they had done poorly. However, knowing what was needed to improve the sales organization and being given the authority to get it done did not necessarily mean that the Representative understood how to lead the entire corporation's sales efforts. Knowledge of what needs to be done and getting the right people to actually do it are two very different activities. Assigning authority does not create leadership.

Many people are unaware that the United States Military was one of the first major institutions to realize that this authority-based leadership style contained a significant weakness found in many other contemporaneous military organizations. By the time of World War II, the personnel at the highest levels of United States Military understood and respected the role of real leadership at the lowest levels of military operation.

High level military administration, at its best, issued clear objectives, set distinct guidelines and provided tools. Operational leadership was recognized at the lowest functional unit. Many writers have attributed the Allies' success of D-Day to the moment-by-moment tactical leadership and decisions made by those directly under fire. Using the same analysis, the German failure was created by tactical units waiting for centralized decisions from the highest levels, paralyzing their ability to undertake timely response.

Establishing pathways of authority is an essential element in a leadership strategy, but it can easily be misinterpreted as a substitute for effective leadership. Success at one level within an organization rarely, if ever, indicates success in a position up the organizational chart that calls for strong leadership skills.

Leadership Not Consensus-ship

The 1970s were dominated by management theories that were strongly influenced by attempts to develop *consensus*. Without intending the result, this process creates groups held hostage by "dictators of veto." Requiring consensus means that the most fear-oriented and negative participants in a group process become the limiting factors for the group's ultimate goals, objectives and final achievements. Leading by consensus reduces your top opportunities and actions to the highest level of activity that every person in the group can accept. Striving for consensus always produces mediocrity or what we like to call, *"The Bland leading the Bland!"*

Beyond core and process, a fundamental definition of many entities is what we find at the edges of shape. It is the edges that often determine how we perceive difference. It is the edges that form the shape of the seal and its beauty – not simply that it is carved from ivory. It is the edges of the seal that differentiate one carver from another. It is at the edges where your operation will touch your customers. Many managers mistakenly begin the process of change at the edges hoping that a functional core and process will emerge. Unfortunately, quite the opposite is true. When core and process are right, effective edges will emerge naturally and serve you well. Always ask first, what is really hiding here?

It is this central task of identifying the true shape and substance, the unique strengths and aspirations of each individual on our broad team that finally allows us to begin to make a new picture of how the entire organization can move forward swiftly and efficiently. It is this profound awareness and focus that prevents us from even considering micro-manipulation. It is this special awareness, respect and valuation of each person's edges that begin to inspire the confidence of others. Keeping this process at the front of our activities ensures that we will move beyond blandness as we begin to assemble the new picture.

While consensus-ship allows the lowest common denominator to establish the highest achievable goals, leadership that operates beyond consensus-ship avoids the ultimate dumbing-down process. The *No Feet In Concrete* process, guiding you to your own leadership strategy, will ensure that you take advantage of the highest possible objectives that reside in your staff and organization.

Leadership is not consensus-ship!

The New Picture

The first task is to use your carving skills on the strengths and opportunities that stand at your door. For a moment, forget the precise commission that you have been assigned. You will easily return to that topic as the picture moves back into focus. Reflecting on your thoughts regarding carving at the end of Chapter 2, consider the following:

- ♦ What is it that your group, company or organization does uniquely well?

- ♦ What achievements is your group expected to accomplish that no one really wants to do? How could these things be accomplished in a new way that would put people on these jobs who would enjoy accomplishing the tasks? Can you live with less than a stellar performance of these tasks? Do you need to recruit new people or face the fact that you won't see profound success here?

♦ What activities can you eliminate that will make things work more smoothly?

♦ And now, how can you communicate the unique, overall objectives of your group or company in a manner that will be absolutely clear to everyone?

It is surprising how rarely entrepreneurial leaders actually communicate these fundamental, larger goals in a clear and unambiguous manner. As redundant as it may seem, it is impossible for people to exercise effective leadership at any level unless they all know exactly where they are headed. Handing someone a map does no good if you don't clearly communicate where you want them to go.

As you begin to complete your new picture, you will want to throw all the old images of org charts into the recycle bin. Pull up the organizational chart for your company on your computer screen. What would your chart communicate about your organization if you handed it to a new hire on their first day? Does it reveal anything (and we mean anything) about how things get done or where to look for genuine support? Does your chart reflect more about lines of authority than it reveals about where real leadership happens in your venture?

Several years ago, while I was conducting an interview with a prospective new employee, she asked if she could see a copy of our organizational chart. I had to actually think for a moment about where we might have a relatively current chart. Fortunately, I was able to borrow one from a colleague and brought it into the meeting and set it on the table.

Her next question was, "Where's the glass line?" I had to admit that I really didn't know what she meant. "The glass line," she repeated in a rather frustrated tone, "How far up the chart do I have to go to get glass in my office?" While I was initially surprised by the question (as the President of the company sitting in an office with very nice floor-to-ceiling windows), I had to admit that this was the most functional use of our org chart I had seen in months.

A new *No Feet In Concrete* picture is **not** just a new org chart . . . far from it. If anything, it is a "func" (function) chart or a "supp" (support) chart.

Put some juice to your hard drive – double click on "orgchart.doc" and take a hard look. Does your organizational chart really center on lines of authority and who does performance reviews for whom (and who the lucky ones are, at the bottom, that don't need to do any – for anyone)? Print a copy of your current chart for posterity. Now . . . close the file, find the file in your directory, highlight it and boldly strike – delete!

Gone is that old chart that said absolutely nothing important, unique or inspiring about your enterprise.

Gone is the expectation that the people below you want to wait for you to make the important decisions for them.

Gone is the flawed assumption that you are managing, directing, controlling the "boxes" below you.

Gone is the assumption that all hell will break loose if you actually forget that, all too often, authority-based strategies quickly get reduced to micro-manipulation. After all, you are operating in an entrepreneurial world – you won't grow or even survive if you are depending upon authority to stay in control.

> *Note: It is highly recommended that you go to your computer's trash bin, find "orgchart.doc," highlight it and hit delete again! We don't want this image to rear its ugly head after we get the real ball rolling.*

True artistic pictures are meant to reveal something about form or feeling. This is a critical element in the process of making the new picture for your staff. In fact, great pictures do not simply represent something. Rather they reveal a new understanding or relationship.

Your new *No Feet In Concrete* picture exists to reveal special ways your company or team works together. Who gets primary work done and what internal and external services are available to make it happen? Who really supports whom? How do you relate to customers? How can you create your new picture so that it includes each and every critical path element of your new leadership process?

It is likely that you will need to create a number of charts to convey your new picture.

Useful Charts

1. Support Diagram

A Support Diagram will indicate how to relate to the various support services and resources that operate inside your enterprise. Where would someone look for help in solving a billing problem? Where would you go to get 64 megs of ram installed in your computer? Who is the right person to talk with regarding a customer who presents a unique opportunity for your product line? Where would you go to get help to develop a quality assurance program in your department? I like to see these diagrams as a picture of all the resources that a person has available to facilitate their particular tasks.

A Support Diagram indicates where a person can look to utilize the range of resources that are available within, and in some cases beyond, your company. This is a valuable chart to hand to a new hire who is looking for ways to quickly get up to speed. Providing a Support Diagram encourages your staff to look beyond their immediate supervisor for internal support services and shows that you know where the real company resources are located and how to deploy them.

We have consciously decided not to include sample diagrams as we did not want to limit the way you would demonstrate how support, leadership and authority should most effectively occur within your team's dynamics.

2. Leadership Diagrams

A Leadership Diagram is helpful to indicate where different styles and patterns of leadership work at various levels. Imagine all the players in your group as puzzle pieces. Each piece includes the name of the person along with the strengths in leadership that the person demonstrates every day.

How would you arrange these puzzle pieces if you tried to indicate how leadership should work on a daily basis? Amazing! When you look at it this way, leaders don't get stacked upon leaders with you at the top as the most skilled leader of all. Leadership happens everywhere and at every level.

Watch for these indicators of effective entrepreneurial leadership:

♦ Some people in your organization will lead by contributing new ideas.

♦ Others lead by motivating people around them to do daily tasks.

♦ Still others lead by creating links between people but rarely get involved in the process itself, much like a catalyst works in a chemical reaction.

♦ Finally, some people lead by providing solutions for others to execute.

Where would someone go to fully understand how your customers think? Where would someone go to find an efficient way to solve an internal problem? Who, within the entire enterprise, could shed light on how to apply a new technology to a customer service need? Who would be the most likely person to head up a "skunk works" solution that would operate outside the normal lines of authority to get a job done on an absolute minimum time schedule? Simply looking up one step on the old _____ chart (notice, it's gone from my computer, too) will not resolve all problems.

Assembling a Leadership Chart with names from all over your organization will be an exceptionally valuable tool for everyone and will show that you understand *how things get done.*

3. Authority Charts

A final consideration is how to represent authority within your venture. Think of a way that you can express to your team how, when and where to find authority. This is not nearly as difficult as it may appear. Where should a person go to get the authority for a purchase order? Who would someone approach if they wanted to change a fundamental message that is being communicated to customers? Who should be informed about a serious Human Resources issue? How should a person communicate a need for new equipment or staff? In many cases the answer is not necessarily the person to whom they directly report, but rather a resource that already has the authority to take direct action.

Where and when does a person have the authority to evaluate a situation and make a decision on their own – only needing to report their action to various people? In which situations does this same person need to look to others for final analysis and decision? Here again, the unclear assignment of authority can dramatically slow the entire process. Unfortunately, many entrepreneurial leaders try to maintain too much authority at the top of an organization, with the result being the loss of good people and the retention of those who move the slowest. Defining authority clearly, and at the lowest functional level, will do wonders, but you need to exercise care to ensure that you assign authority to those who have the tools to exercise it carefully.

Don't confuse authority with initiative. You always want to encourage initiative, but you want to be careful not to let people get "out over their skis" when you assign authority.

Most of the time we function as leaders in some situations and followers in others. There is no more dysfunctional leader than a person who attempts to maintain a leadership posture, even when they are well outside of their personal competency maps. Equally dysfunctional is the leader who is threatened by the leadership of others. If you are the key player in your venture, do you recognize the times and areas where others lead? If you step in at this point, these valuable people will either stop leading or find another opportunity to contribute their valuable leadership, leaving you with a group of weak-minded followers.

The point here is that you need leadership at every level of your company. Watch for various styles of functional leadership and reinforce them at every opportunity – even when you feel you don't have the time for it.

> Reinforcing real leadership (not blind authority) is your key job when you are making this new picture.

Getters, Doers and Leaders

Now that you are beginning to make your new picture, how are you doing for "getters" and "doers"? Some people are naturally focused on bringing work to the table, while others seem more comfortable with the process of getting work done. Still other people really know how to lead the process at various levels.

To ensure a smooth result, be sure that you have staff in the right spots, functioning where they really do thrive. If you have getters in spots where they are expected to be doers, you will want to move them to a place where they will be better used and, no doubt, more happy. Your carving conversations with your staff will reveal this quickly.

A great example of this process happened at a gathering of our Marketing Managers who met to discuss their role in the picture at Panagraph. After some discussion, I boldly told them that they were not expected to do any selling, nor did our Business Development group want them to sell anything. The message was that we wanted them to keep their focus on leading accounts and let the Business Development group do their job.

The response was both disbelief and relief. They thought that they were responsible to sell products and services to their clients. It was clear that while they didn't really **want** to be selling (they really wanted to provide services), they felt that we expected it to be part of their job. Their focus was to lead their clients to the most effective marketing results possible – not selling products and ideas.

I explained to them that when they tried to develop new business they were taking the fun out of the work of our Business Development group. Giving these sales pros even room-temperature leads was like throwing steaks to lions. They loved it. The Business Development team didn't want to provide marketing services. They wanted get out and find valuable opportunities that would allow the marketing managers to work their magic.

You may find that you have people on your staff doing things that make them uncomfortable in their skin. Regardless of what is included in their job description, they won't be effective unless it is part of their "seal." As soon as you see people in the wrong positions with parts of their job descriptions that don't fit, you need to act swiftly to retain (or regain) their confidence and support.

Expanding the Picture

To be a leader you need to lead every vital component of your success, not just those that would have been on your old _____ chart. How do you represent the relationships of valued suppliers? How do your customers fit into your organization's big picture? What kind of leadership should be provided to consultants and others who provide valuable services to your company?

> For many years, Panagraph has served a client whose engineering and manufacturing facilities are located more than 175 miles from our home office. After producing several years of valuable marketing support services with our staff traveling to their offices, the President of the company realized that, with the exception of one person, no one on their staff had been to Panagraph's main facility. Upon this realization, his comment to me was that Panagraph was one of their most valuable suppliers, and he immediately expressed personal interest in visiting our office.
>
> My first response to him was that we would need to "clean out the barn" before he could come

and visit. After a good laugh, we agreed that it would be our pleasure to have him come to meet the rest of our staff.

During his trip, the President emphasized that his company had come to consider Panagraph as an extension of their organization. He related that he appreciated the commitment our staff demonstrated in the work they did for them. The times that his staff members and Sales Representatives have taken to come to our home office has always served to inspire Panagraph to redouble its efforts to provide outstanding work for them.

This ongoing effort serves as a powerful example of extending a company picture far beyond your real estate and your internal lines of authority, linking each and every vital segment of the company's success. Today, this company is proud to include both Panagraph and its employees as vital elements in its operational processes.

Moving the boundaries of your picture beyond your company borders will indicate your understanding of precisely how you depend upon outside sources for your success. This practice will send a valuable message to your staff about how you expect them to deal with these resources, not as adversaries, but as assets. Communicating this relationship to critical path suppliers will highlight your need for solid performance from them and let them know how they directly contribute (or fail to contribute) to your ongoing success.

Summing It Up

The first part of this chapter suggested that organizational charts can easily be confused as authority charts. It is not functional to mistake authority for leadership.

As you introduce your new picture, you will want to highlight real entrepreneurial leadership and avoid the boat anchor of consensus-ship.

If you are going to achieve dramatic results you need to make a clear new broad-based picture with many different images and diagrams to communicate how support, leadership and authority should operate within your organization.

The new picture of your organization is not just a map of performance reviews. Your image will include the ways that you interact with customers, suppliers and other outside resources, including the leadership that you depend upon from them. It will be a clear illustration of exactly where you want to go, how to get there and what outside opportunities drive your corporate goals and objectives.

Questions and Actions

1. Take a good look at your present _____ chart and what it communicates. Talk with other people in your group to determine exactly what information resides within this chart.

2. Make a list of the things that you would like to communicate to a new hire or member of your group about how your organization operates. Try your list out on others to determine if you are covering all the important information. What was the most controversial? What was unnecessary? What elements got the most discussion and why? Be sure to utilize as much of this feedback as possible.

3. Try your hand at some graphic images that catch the unique spirit of how things work in your enterprise. Try to include the concepts of support, leadership and authority in your diagrams.

4. Test out your work. Present your materials to someone "above" you in your organization and watch their reaction. Don't be surprised if they are stunned by your initiative and insight. Some people have trouble thinking outside the boxes.

5. Now it's time to test out your picture in the real world. Try it out on a few people at a time to give yourself a chance to utilize their feedback.

CHAPTER 4
Setting The Jugular Issue

"The problem that I face continually is that people want me to make their decisions for them. They know what we are trying to accomplish and what their job is, but they seem unable to step to the plate and make the tough decisions without me. If I had the time to get all the information and experience needed to make all the decisions, I wouldn't need them on the payroll. Besides, if we were all coming to the same conclusions it would mean that none of us was really thinking."

- Making Decisions Is Not Leadership

- The Jugular Issue

- Avoiding the Obvious

- Simple Tests

- Changing the Jugular Issue

- Barriers to Change

- Ideas to Reinforce Change

- Commitment Speeds Change

Making Decisions Is Not Leadership

When you ask people what job they would really like to do, the quick answer is often, "The one in the corner office." And, if you ask what it is about that job that is so outwardly appealing, the answer usually is, "I want to be the one that makes all the decisions."

Such is the perception of leadership – leaders are the ones who make all the decisions. In reality, decision making controlled at the highest levels of an organization is yet another classic boat anchor of successful leadership. If entrepreneurial leadership is to break through this barrier, we cannot confuse leadership with simply making all of the decisions.

If you feel yourself making too many decisions and you are ready to take advantage of the strengths of entrepreneurial leadership, you can be sure that your role will change and you will find yourself in a much more satisfying environment.

Most leaders intuitively know that they shouldn't make all the decisions. In many cases, they both resent it and report that it takes more time out of their workday than it should. They know that it is far more efficient to delegate decision making, but they often convey that they are unable to get others to make the right decisions or even get them to make decisions at all.

This problem is often seen in non-profit organizations. People strive to be in decision-making positions and then quickly burn out in an attempt to do it all. Authority to make decisions is first delegated, then expected, then taken for granted and finally resented by all parties. Why does this happen so frequently in so many venues? What is it about this entrepreneurial tendency that leads to this familiar paradigm?

The answer is often the same. Frequently we confuse leadership with final decision making and authority. In reality, a more functional leadership model would conclude that true entrepreneurial leadership is the opportunity to *delegate* decision making and authority. The big opportunity for a fast-paced leader in an entrepreneurial environment is not whether to delegate but *how* to entrust these functions to others and still keep your department together and moving in the right direction.

> In the late 1990s when Panagraph began its extraordinary new growth cycle, we began by hiring a number of exceptional "GenXers" who entered the company with both outstanding skills and clearly applicable experience. These were not apprentices who needed preparation and training. Rather, they were focused and ready to perform well beyond our goals and expectations. These new members of our Panagraph leadership team were ready to create radical success. As President, I was commissioned to ensure that this new talent moved in the right direction to support our corporate goals.

> The trick was to maintain functional feedback to our entire staff without controlling or micro-managing each person's contribution. If I began down the road of micro-management, I would have cut off the precise contribution that proved to turn average performance into incredible success. The result was well beyond the goals that we had established and far beyond anything that was even seen as possible by our Board of Directors.

The real key was that while I did delegate decision making and gave up a big slice of authority, I never gave up my responsibility to set the guidelines and priorities for how decisions were to be made.

We refer to this process as **"Setting the Jugular Issue."**

The Jugular Issue

Here's the key to forever letting go of a significant boat anchor. Setting the Jugular Issue for your organization means that you respect the ability of those you lead to conduct useful situation analyses and make solid decisions. It also communicates your confidence in their ability to make the right decisions. It indicates that you will support their decisions as long as they utilize the guidelines that you have established.

> *The Jugular Issue is the insight that you provide that will help your entire enterprise cut away the most of what isn't absolutely essential, removing the fundamental barriers and releasing the vital energy that is hiding within. It is the final factor for your staff to consider after they have applied their best analyses and looked methodically at the full range of possible decisions.*

Your team members apply the Jugular Issue as they make their final decisions to move forward without requiring further input from you. Utilizing the Jugular Issue, they will be confident that their decisions will fit within your current, critical path objectives. It is the final test and measure for your staff to consider as they exercise their authority and make vital decisions on their own.

A mid-sized service firm at a *No Feet In Concrete* seminar carried out one of the most memorable applications of the Jugular Issue. After attempting for more than an hour to define the Jugular Issue for their company, the President boldly stated that they would make the most profitable long-term gains if they focused more clearly on their most profitable accounts.

When his staff asked the President to state it as a Jugular Issue he quickly replied, "Every decision and action that we make in the future needs to help us focus on profitable work. If it doesn't – don't do it!" The President stood up and wrote on the board:

Focus Every Decision on Profitable Work.

Without a word being spoken one of the members of the management staff walked dramatically to the phone and brought it back to the table. From memory he dialed a number and began a short discussion with what was obviously one of their company's accounts. He candidly mentioned that he felt that their company would be unable to give them the proper amount of attention in the near future. To the ultimate amazement of all in attendance and with all members of the management staff listening, he quickly addressed the problem with the client and suggested that there was a smaller firm in Silicon Valley that could likely do a very credible job for them. He continued by saying that he would like to arrange a three-way meeting with both the client and the new firm to ensure an efficient hand off.

None of the attendees could believe what they were hearing. They all knew that this was a small client, but a large anchor for the firm. At one time or another they had all complained that this client had demanded a disproportionate and unprofitable amount of time.

In less than five minutes it was over. When the staff member pushed the button to disconnect everyone stood and cheered.

The President was very serious about the need to focus. The staff member had wrestled with the decision for weeks, but now had a clear guideline and mandate to act. Hanging on to unprofitable work had become the boat anchor that deterred growth in both new clients and overall profitability! Within weeks, the Jugular Issue immediately took hold and became the guiding principle for the management staff for many months, until it became a solid strength of their entire company.

It is surprising how pervasive and effective a Jugular Issue can be if it is chosen well. For the above company, it became the hallmark of decisions well beyond its management staff. The business development staff began to focus their efforts on what the service providers had defined as profitable accounts, rather than just looking for business by what they saw on the other side of their windshields. Internal service providers were encouraged because they began to only see clients that they could serve well. Bidding became easier because they only bid jobs that they totally understood and to customers that needed the work. The simple statement of the *Jugular Issue* by the President, which began at the seminar, became the powerful symbol of commanding change and movement toward new growth.

One of my often-quoted examples of a well-working Jugular Issue is from a personal experience with one of our staff members. Our office manager was talking with me about how she would like to address a problem within our administrative team. I had asked her to look for ways to speed up the billing process.

This young staff member began by explaining several unnecessary steps that had been utilized for years. After she displayed a full understanding of problem, I quickly (and wrongly) interrupted her before she began to present her ideas by defending the current process, based on my "twenty-five years of experience."

Because we were in the midst of substantive growth, I had set the following Jugular Issue:

Be Sure That Whatever We Do Creates Scaleable and Elegant Process.

Delightfully, the first words out of her mouth boldly demonstrated her understanding of our current Jugular Issue. "Doing it the same old way," she asserted, "will not create a 'scaleable or elegant process' – we're just going to continue to be buried by a job that really doesn't need nearly as much time as we give it!"

You've got to love that. Your administrative staff holds you accountable for your own Jugular Issue. Needless to say she had a valuable, scaleable and elegant solution to our billing barrier, and I was delighted to see her implement her plan . . . and it worked well.

Jugular Issues apply just as well to daily living and family activities as they do in the workplace. What is holding you back personally? Forget what those self-improvement gurus are selling you on TV about what you need to do. Look within – what's really hiding there? What do you need to cut away to reveal your true self? Don't try to push away what isn't "seal" – just let it go. You don't need it. What you have is enough if you don't let the unessential get in the way or cloud the picture. Post your Jugular Issue on your mirror, and be sure to apply it to everything you do. You will be pleased with the results, and the people around you will quickly begin to develop deep confidence in you and your leadership abilities.

Avoiding the Obvious

It is important to note that a Jugular Issue is NOT a recycled version of the tired practice of creating a mission statement. Jugular Issues do not attempt to define anything – they exist only to be a final guide for decision making when choosing options and activities.

We have all sat through long and tedious sessions that were no more than truncated efforts to establish some elementary focus and definition for a company or organization. These overused and largely ignored exercises were deeply rooted in consensus-ship and rarely, if ever, produced clarified direction or measurable results. They nearly all included words such as "the finest," "customer driven," "world class" and "total quality." In reality, these efforts rarely revealed anything new about how to make decisions nor did it drive a company to a new position. The exercise also assumed that it was the people "down the chart" that needed guidance, focus and direction – a bold conjecture at best. In many cases these people who are often placed at the bottom of the chart know what an organization is, in fact, doing.

Likewise, a Jugular Issue is not simply a final goal to be achieved and should not be confused with discovering the hidden seal in the ivory. The Jugular Issue ensures that we will carve away precisely what will finally create the highest achievements possible. The Jugular Issue should be utilized to firmly guide each carving stroke as we lead toward stated goals.

Simple Tests

+ If you conclude (after a few trial balloons with a trusted member of your staff) that your Jugular Issue is obvious to all, then you haven't identified a true Jugular Issue. Your **Jugular** Issue should be a driver at the point of critical decisions – a final test to ensure that a particular decision will be in concert with those essential objectives that will break barriers and ensure success. Jugular Issues are not generalized overall goals to be reached.

♦ Does your Jugular Issue limit some activities and decisions and reinforce others? If it doesn't provide this limiting function, it's not going to provide the vital elements necessary to free you from making decisions that others are able to make.

♦ Is your Jugular Issue being quoted back to you? If a staff member presents an idea to you and makes the final pitch utilizing your Jugular Issue – you've got a winner.

Changing the Jugular Issue

Jugular Issues may need to be changed at any time. If you continue to utilize your Jugular Issue you will find that it will become internalized and you will achieve the essential components that it is intended to address. When you begin to feel that change is happening and that your Jugular Issue has been internalized, it's time to take a careful look at the big picture. Again, here are some questions to consider that will help determine the appropriate time to change the Jugular Issue:

♦ Has your Jugular Issue become completely internalized and part of your overall process?

♦ What's holding back dramatic success now?

♦ Are there new internal issues that have become excuses for the lack of forward movement?

♦ What issues dominate the conversation when you meet with your team?

♦ Do you see "choke points" in your process?

♦ Are there external issues that seem to get constant attention?

♦ Are you getting any consistent signals from customers or those you serve?

♦ Have you noticed any subtle changes in corporate culture that point to internal stress?

If you see light in any of the above questions you may want to take a fresh look at your Jugular Issue. It may be time to make a change. In reality, this is your most important task as you begin to make your best entrepreneurial leadership skills work for you. It is your skill addressing vital questions and setting the Jugular Issue that qualifies you as an effective leader. Ask the above questions and then think insight, analysis and inspiration. You'll soon be on your way to a new Jugular Issue.

Look beyond the obvious. What is at the root of all the current input you are receiving? Where is the common ground? Finally, what new guideline can you present that will break the biggest barriers and carve away the most of what is not seal?

Barriers to Change

The first time that you actually change the Jugular Issue you may find that your staff will not react as quickly as you would like. It is important to understand some of the reasons why this may happen.

1. Your staff has finally internalized the last Jugular Issue and is beginning to act on it instinctively. They have been using it long enough to make it a vital component in their decision-making process.

2. The Jugular Issue has been helpful as they made decisions, carving away barriers and establishing a more effective way of working with the people they lead.

3. Your Jugular Issue has become an instrument of your staff's personal success. This is no small issue as they have seen themselves as more wired into the overall success of the process.

4. Finally, your staff will identify your Jugular Issue with real forward movement. Seeing your commitment to the Jugular Issue and sensing its effect will have generated powerful, positive feelings. In some cases we have seen a Jugular Issue generate the first positive movement in an organization in a long period of time. Your staff may have identified the current Jugular Issue with this initial positive movement.

In reality, all of the above results, which you have sensed from your initial use of a Jugular Issue, will become the basis of your new Jugular Issue.

Ideas to Reinforce Change

Here are some ways that our seminar participants have re-set a new Jugular Issue. (Thanks to each of you who have sent us your ideas):

1. Before setting a new Jugular Issue, one leader meets with his team and explains to them that he is pleased with the way they have used the Jugular Issue to guide their total effort. He asks them to recount examples to the rest of the group about how they used it and what decisions have been affected by their use of the Jugular Issue. He tries to

cite examples of ways that he has seen valuable growth as a result of these good decisions. After this conversation, he states the new Jugular issue and asks for feedback from his management staff.

2. Another group mentioned that they use small office signs to convey a change of a Jugular Issue. When they want to make a change, they simply make small, two-sided signs that are placed in various spaces around the office. Without fanfare, these colorful signs become a point of conversation. Team members take it upon themselves to explain the concept and use of the Jugular Issue to new members. After these informal discussions, the entire department understands what the Jugular Issue is and how to use it.

3. Another example came from a small company who finds that changing the Jugular Issue is a good excuse to create a fun new company toy. One example that got big response was stress balls with the Jugular Issue printed on them. Some even ended up in the hands of customers.

4. One group uses clever screen savers that are installed on every computer overnight.

5. We generally have our design department create posters with the initial Jugular Issue for first time *No Feet In Concrete* seminar participants. Four or five well designed framed posters, strategically positioned, will definitely initiate conversation.

Commitment Speeds Change

Finding unique ways to initiate a new Jugular Issue should definitely be part of the fun, but it will only work if you see it as your primary duty to communicate the full range of what it means. Even if you have a well-stated Jugular Issue, it still takes some effort to articulate just what you mean and how profoundly you expect it to be used.

The first time you use the concept of the Jugular Issue you will want to initiate a discussion covering both overall definitions and examples as to how you expect your department to use the concept. After this first session, people may still come to you and ask you to make decisions for them. This may be because you have expected them to come to you in the past. They need to see you working a new system. When they approach you, listen carefully to their concerns, and then ask them how those issues relate to the Jugular Issue. If you have selected a perfect catalytic Jugular Issue, they will apply it immediately and discover that you are serious about your new process. You will display respect in their ability to make good decisions. Each time this happens it will reinforce your deep commitment to your unique, new way of leading. They will immediately see your total commitment and how your new leadership process will:

1. Help them move more quickly through the decision-making process.

2. Help them to carve away unnecessary grief and activities.

3. Keep their focus on forward movement in a positive direction.

The most important point here is that you utilize the Jugular Issue in conversations with your staff each time you encounter them wrestling with decisions. Your personal and methodical utilization and verbal reinforcement of the Jugular Issue is a critical component in speeding the time to useful adoption.

As you continue to use the Jugular Issue in your work with your staff, you will find that the Jugular Issue will soon be seen as synonymous with your commitment to your new custom-designed, personally crafted leadership strategy. It will be focused deeply upon real progress, rooted in personal strengths and, most importantly, will be accomplished with no one's feet in concrete – not theirs, not yours and not anyone's in your entire enterprise.

Summing It Up

We opened the chapter discussing the differences between daily decision making and leadership in an entrepreneurial world. Leadership at its best is a process of developing a big picture and finding an effective way to delegate decision making at every point possible.

By setting a Jugular Issue and communicating it clearly to all participants in your process, you can provide a guiding resource which ensures that decisions will address critical issues in your process. It will also serve to ensure that decisions remove the significant barriers that hold back dramatic growth. Your ability to translate your insight into a useful Jugular Issue will demonstrate a profound understanding of the overall process. If you follow this process and develop a unique Jugular Issue, your insight will be recognized and it will quickly develop confidence in your ability to lead, regardless of your current position in an organization.

In all cases you want to steer clear of reinforcing the tired practice of writing a mission statement or setting new goals and objectives. These activities are often mistaken for setting a Jugular Issue. Often based on consensus-ship, they will only serve to put your feet in concrete and prevent any kind of effective leadership in an entrepreneurial world.

We offered some questions that would serve as guidelines to know when it was time to change the Jugular Issue. These questions also revealed how you would discover the foundation for your next Jugular Issue.

When Jugular Issues become internalized it can be difficult to change to a new one. There are many ways to reinforce a new

Jugular Issue, but the two basic elements that you will need to utilize are (1) identify and reinforce where the old Jugular issue had been used and (2) do something dramatic (and fun) to make your point. Your ongoing commitment, demonstrated by articulating the new Jugular Issue wherever you see people struggling with decisions, will speed the successful use of a new Jugular Issue.

The Jugular Issue will become the most important indication of your commitment to the development of a unique leadership style for your organization. It will be the single most visible element that you can use to demonstrate that you are not trying to implement yet another "canned" theory to manage their work.

Utilizing a well chosen Jugular Issue frees up your group to confidently make critical decisions and lead others as you monitor the process. It also allows you to look for the right time to continue the process by issuing a new Jugular Issue.

Questions and Actions

1. Talk with another member of your staff regarding the most discussed change that could fuel dramatic new growth for your organization. Make a short list of all the related elements that affect the issue. Who does it affect? How and why has this particular issue affected the entire operation? What would need to happen to make this critical element of new growth become a fuel for change?

2. Try working this into a Jugular Issue. Will this serve as a useful final test that would guide vital decision making as your staff brings the new picture online?

3. What types of decisions would your Jugular Issue prevent? What kinds of decisions would it support?

4. Make a small triangular "table tent" with your Jugular Issue on it. Put it on your desk and see what discussion in creates. Is it sharp enough to create solid decisions in concert with your big picture? If it's just a goal that just feels good but doesn't carve away at the process, send it to the circular file – it's time for a new table tent.

5. Be sure that your Jugular Issue is simple enough to understand so that you can write it up on a board and your staff will instinctively know how to use it.

6. Finally, if you have made it this far – give it a shot. Be sure to let your staff know what you are trying to do. You are creating a unique leadership style, and you will support *their* initiative and decision making as long as they apply your Jugular Issue. Don't resist refining your Jugular Issue – your staff will likely give you good input.

7. Keep carving, questioning, making the big picture and articulating your Jugular Issue. Your obvious commitment to the total process will speed you toward that unique strategy that we promised in the introduction of this book.

CHAPTER 5
The New Non-Paradigm: Elements to Consider

"When we began to use our own new leadership process, we saw an entirely new paradigm in the way we worked together. Beginning with real basics and making our own strategy created a real sense of efficiency that brought new energy to our entire department. We discovered new strengths every day and put them to good use."

- Process Not Product

- A Clear Focus

- No Pushing on Rocks

- Only Strengths and Opportunities

- Off-Course Correction

- Internalize It or It Won't Work

Process Not Product

No doubt you are beginning to see the boat anchor insidiously hiding in leadership theories that are dominated by goals and objectives. Leading by simply setting goals and holding people accountable could be easily accomplished and measured with a $50 software program. We all know how to cook numbers and avoid responsibility when we are assigned goals and objectives that we don't have the skill, drive or desire to accomplish. This type of management is a few courses short of rocket science. No need for any high-paying jobs here.

Leadership is an entirely different endeavor. Unlike achieving a goal, leadership demands that we continually create and display a process. Focusing upon goals is internally inefficient as it assumes some kind of linear progression of development within the progress of an organization. In reality a fast-moving, entrepreneurial enterprise is driven by a non-linear, parallel process that does not respond to one goal stacked upon the next. Even when an organization has a clearly defined set of objectives, it can become lost in process if it attempts to climb one short-term mountain after another. Your staff doesn't need a long series of sequential, singular objectives; they need to be set free to work as part of an ongoing big picture.

> *Carve your assets. Make the picture. Show how the pieces fit together. Control the process with only one sharp Jugular Issue. Fuel the process with commitment. And watch dramatic success happen.*

What you are creating is a process that continually refreshes itself. Focusing on individual goals and objectives is back to square-one type micro-manipulation. Leadership is practical process in action – constantly moving and changing style and method as your enterprise moves forward. Each moment of growth requires a slightly new strategy and will challenge you to flex and grow with the process.

So often, just as we get things going right, something happens that questions the process and commands our immediate attention. When we lead, especially in the ever-quickening entrepreneurial environment in which we find ourselves, the very achievement of success creates changes in the overall organization. Success creates new opportunities. We either respond quickly or we begin to see the change as a threat. This is the reason that many people are afraid of success. They don't want to be accountable for the change that it inherently demands.

The fearless entrepreneurial leader is neither afraid of the achievement of short-term success nor the changes that success demands. Confidence is not necessarily knowing all the answers yourself, since the most powerful responses to many opportunities may very well come from the people who see you as their leader. Confidence is created by the assurance that the *process*, which you continually create and utilize, will dependably produce powerful results. Utilizing your personally crafted leadership methods, tailored to your organization and born of its deepest strengths, will work in every case. If you have the right people in the right spots and keep yourself focused on process (not micro-managing their goals) your staff will deeply appreciate your confidence, value your leadership and perform beyond your wildest expectations. This focus on process is not rocket science, but it does take continual discipline, attention and commitment.

A Clear Focus

There is a popular story about a survey that was conducted among the members of a Yale graduating class in the 1950s. The graduates were polled several times during their lives to assess their well-being, happiness and prosperity. Among other interesting insights, one, in particular, seemed to prove how important personal focus could be for future success. During the first survey, 3 percent of the graduates indicated that they had developed written goals for their lives. After thirty years that same 3 percent was worth more money than the rest of the other 97 percent together.

Focus. Written and internalized **FOCUS!**

There is a delightful Zen saying that brings an enjoyable expansion to the understanding of focus:

Sit, Walk or Run – Just don't wobble.

Without focus life quickly becomes a series of constant distractions. A completely internalized sense of your big picture is the foundation of focus. Focus upon an internalized map and destination makes the journey so much easier. Without clear focus you can easily become a victim of other people's programming.

There will be a never-ending list of others who are ready to hand you a map with their destination circled in red. Your own focus is **power.** Power rooted in clear focus will become an internal inspiration for you. It will also, without question, become a source of inspiration and success for others.

Distraction is the bane of great leadership. It is confusing to those you lead and becomes a major barrier in your effort to communicate both your big picture and your Jugular Issue. No one gravitates toward a leader who sends a distracted, confused and unclear message. Distraction prevents powerful leadership. Focus creates muscle and strength.

Focus is the central key to using your Jugular Issue. Focusing daily light on your Jugular Issue will help others around you see the power of focus. Like many other leadership skills, focus is learned. One of the gifts of maturity is to continually learn how to focus more effectively.

> As I began to write this book I had trouble getting the first chapter finalized and ready for others to read. The process became more and more frustrating until I realized that I was attempting to add the writing of the book to my daily activities as President of our company. It wasn't so much that I didn't have the time to write, but other priorities and activities constantly distracted me from my commitment to get it done on schedule. The company was growing at a pace that kept my attention, and that very growth often held its own intoxicating grip on my daily attention.
>
> A further complication included my commitment to our accepted Jugular Issue and the ongoing articulation of that issue to everyone in our company. That was my job – setting the Jugular Issue and articulating it everywhere:

Do everything to create
a scaleable and elegant process!

While this Jugular issue had served the company well in guiding its growth, what I needed was my own Jugular Issue to drive my writing. It didn't need to be scaleable or elegant; it needed to guide my daily decisions regarding what to do and what to avoid doing.

After a couple of days and some discussion, my new Jugular Issue popped out of my laptop screen where I was making notes:

Simplify and Focus

Here was the real test that I needed as I made daily decisions. Did what I was considering simplify what I was doing, and was I avoiding all possible distractions? If the answer was yes to both, it went on my priority list – if it didn't it got eliminated. Within a few days I was ready to let go of the first chapter. It felt like I had let go of a boat anchor that could have been used for an aircraft carrier.

My coworkers knew how to approach me and immediately began to help me simplify what I did in relation to both the book and the company. And further, they respected the time that I had assigned to writing because they knew that I had *Focus* in my Jugular Issue.

Typical of a Jugular Issue, it carved away those things that were not precisely what I needed to get the job done. The book was there in my head, but I needed everyone to help me apply my Jugular Issue to help get it into my laptop.

After a few days the director of the No Feet In Concrete team began to quote my Jugular Issue back to me when she saw me get distracted with daily unessentials. A sure sign that a Jugular Issue is working well.

No Pushing on Rocks

It's time to discuss the value of the time-worn process of SWOT analyses. For years people have conducted what was referred to as a situation analysis before they embarked on a new project or venture. It carried some inherent weaknesses that, in and of itself, held back progress. We used to begin a situation analysis by organizing input and discussion around four concepts.

Strengths   Weaknesses   Opportunities   Threats

Below each concept we made a list of all the items, both internal and external, that came within these categories. Generally beginning with brainstorming (a fascinating word for the process), long lists were developed and discussed.

Most of the time these charts had a few items listed under strengths and opportunities, a few more listed under threats and many more listed under weaknesses. Often, the discussions finally centered on weaknesses because they were seen as the most likely components that could be changed. Opportunities and threats were often seen as "out there" in the marketplace, while strengths were considered fixed assets (both physical and personal) and were common reasons for the discussion.

The analysis continued with the following premise: Eliminate weaknesses, neutralize or eliminate threats, and use your strengths to respond to opportunities.

Why was it that so many times we got lost in the "weaknesses" section? In his book *Zen Mind, Beginner's Mind,* Suzuki refers to this kind of experience as "pushing on rocks." Often, the more we talk about a weakness, the closer we get to it, the stronger it feels, and the more it seems to even actively resist movement. The harder we push, the more credible and defined the problem becomes. Lengthy discussion can often confirm and strengthen a weakness rather than give us any tools to get beyond it. Most certainly, credibility and attention assigned to a weakness will never generate energy or confidence. Just talking about a weakness will not make it go away. Understanding is not eliminating.

As leaders, one of our biggest assignments when looking at the opportunities that present themselves to our ventures is to always discuss weaknesses or threats in the context of a solution. That is really the only reason you discuss the problem in the first place. Without a solution tied to a threat or weakness, it's just a gripe session.

Gripe sessions are always dysfunctional because they stop the process by pushing on rocks. While it may temporarily feel good to vent a bit in an attempt to get your feelings out, if you stop there you will always conclude that nothing good came of the discussion. Long discussions about threats will have the same effect: assign increased strength to the threat and diffuse energy and confidence needed to address the issue creatively. Airing weaknesses and threats without continually requiring associated possible solutions rarely, if ever, motivates a profound response.

Only Strengths and Opportunities

On many occasions people have asked why one of the central *No Feet In Concrete* principles often involves the elimination of any discussion of threats and weaknesses. How can you operate by ignoring threats and weaknesses? Is this yet another rendition of Norman Vincent Peale's "power of positive thinking?" The answer is a resounding "No" because we have no intention of avoiding threats or weaknesses. Instead, if we follow the above discipline carefully, the process will begin to reveal the strengths and opportunities that are associated with the weaknesses and threats.

We were recently pleased to host a mid-sized manufacturing company's top leaders at a *No Feet In Concrete* seminar. During their discussions about the strengths and opportunities hiding in their services, we asked that they not discuss any weaknesses or threats. After some discussion it became clear that there was one very powerful topic that they wanted to talk about but felt that they were not being allowed to do so.

Finally, one member of the staff asked why we were not allowing them to discuss the negatives. "How are we going to move forward without discussing these issues?" he asked. The entire group identified one specific issue as a significant impediment to growth. We responded by asking if they had discussed this issue before. "Certainly," was the response. "We have discussed it to death, but we just get angry and discouraged and move on to other topics. And, I'll bet if we discuss it now it will just start all over again."

They had been stifled by a quality problem for several months. Their new, high-profile product was not working well in the field, experiencing a random crashing problem. It had begun to shed poor light on the entire company. The timing for a product failure could not have been worse. They had just announced that this new product was a direct replacement for their older and well-accepted product. People stopped buying their cash cow and began to wait until they got their quality problem fixed. Sales were slowing dramatically.

Engineering blamed manufacturing – manufacturing blamed engineering and even purchasing – and no viable progress had been made to address the issue. To make matters worse, the in-house sales staff was initially told that the problem didn't exist and was probably operator error, which did not enhance customer relations. Now they began to lose their credibility with both customers and distributors. The problem dragged on for months and no one accepted responsibility for the problem or its solution. Meanwhile, while it had been "talked to death," no real progress had been made.

As the seminar proceeded, we suggested that they rephrase the threat to read as an opportunity. What was the opportunity hiding there within this weakness and threat?

At first they had a tough time making the process work. Finally, the sales manager said, "If we had a product that didn't crash at critical times, we would make a ton of money!" A good start. The second attempt initiated real progress, "If we could just talk about the problem openly and avoid everyone being defensive, we would be a hell of a lot more likely to find a solution!" The third try, from the financial officer, hit the nail on the head.

"We have the best product on the market and everyone wants it. We have the best engineers in the world; we have a strong distribution system; and we have a solid customer base. We owe it to our customers and our staff to stop wasting our time placing blame and work together to solve this problem – now."

After a few moments of silence it was obvious that the normally quiet financial officer had struck a powerful, motivating chord with the entire group. It was the first time anyone admitted that they were at a standstill because they had limited their discussion to fixing blame. Someone had made a mistake – the product was not working correctly – and finally, in a few moments of insight, they were all focused on solving the problem, instead of ducking blame.

In a few weeks the problem was discovered. A minor design flaw existed in a critical buy-out component that had never caused a problem in other applications. The new product, as designed, depended heavily upon a specific feature that did not work well and caused the product to crash. As it turned out, one of the engineers who worked on the product had a good hunch about the problem from the beginning. However, the R&D supervisor directed him not to pursue it because it would just open a can of worms for the department and they were buried with other work. And, he said he was "sure" that the component was doing what it was designed to do.

Requiring your staff to bring problems to you in the form of opportunities has another powerful element hiding within the process. When you have been in a leadership position, how often has a staff member come to you with a problem and somehow, in the process, ended up putting the monkey on your back before slipping quietly out the door? If you allow others to complain without solutions, you actually encourage them to leave the problems on your desk to resolve.

If you find yourself in this position and wisely require your staff to rephrase their problem as an opportunity guided by your Jugular Issue, you will do three productive things:

1. You will *lead* them, not *do* for them.

2. You will require them to think through to a proper solution that will strengthen your operation because it is in concert with your Jugular Issue. They are closest to the issue and will probably be able to propose the best solution.

3. You will succeed in not allowing them to put the monkey on your back and communicate to them that it is not acceptable to do so.

> *"My computer crashes two or three times every day – I can't get done what everyone expects me to do to stay within our group timeline!"*

> You feel the monkey moving toward you. You begin to reach dramatically for your red SOS rubber stamp and inkpad, looking longingly at their forehead.

> *"OOPS, I mean, if my computer worked right I could stay within my group's schedule."*

> You hesitate slightly, indicating that they are on the right path.

> *"What I really mean is that it is extremely frustrating when my computer crashes and I have to redo my work – it puts me behind the power curve. If my computer worked well and I didn't have to redo the work, I would be a top producer and a heck of a lot happier. If the Jugular Issue is to create "Scaleable and Elegant Process" then the I.T. department should put a ton more RAM in my computer, get me a new one, or do something else that will solve the problem."*

You put down the inkpad but still hold on to the stamp.

"The I.T. department will know how to solve the problem. They will be able do this without me having to make a big deal about it or get an approval from you or anyone, right?"

You put down the inkpad and smile.

Problem solved. No whining. No monkey moving from one back to another. Utilizing your SOS rubber stamp, you have provided perfect leadership without uttering a single word.

When you require all items to be brought to you or your staff meetings as opportunities and strengths, you avoid pushing on rocks and lead others by requiring them to identify solutions and maintain responsibility for progress in their area.

Off-Course Correction

Off-course denial will inherently prevent on-course correction. You may want to consider a heavier focus on off-course correction rather than require your staff to report that they are precisely on schedule and task.

Leaders often focus a good deal of their attention upon keeping people on course and on task. However, many leaders who maintain this position actually create more problems than they avoid. As a matter of fact, the emphasis on being on course can create the exact problem that it intends to resolve.

In aviation, how often are pilots precisely on course in their three-dimensional medium? The answer – never. Aviation is a constant state of correction. All of the instruments on board are there to tell pilots when and how they are not on-course and what to do about it. Good pilots always assume that they need to make constant corrections and are never satisfied with their precise position while in flight. They always assume that they are off-course in some small way. Winds change, temperatures change, altitude assignments change, engine settings change – all requiring constant attention to continual off-course correction.

Finally, pilots are taught that if all of their navigational equipment is dead center, indicating that they are precisely on course, there is a high probability that their battery is dead!

Too many leadership and strategic plans are designed in a manner that assumes everyone is, and always will be, on course, unless reported otherwise. All too often we make plans according to exactly what we need to do to be on course, rarely thinking about or planning what to do when we are off course and who else could profit from that knowledge.

Success is often measured and reinforced by how much time we are on our pre-planned course. What would change if we measured and reinforced how much of the time we are **in sync** with everyone else working on a project? Would more effort be spent communicating and talking about course correction, rather than trying to convince co-workers and "supervisors" that we were right on course? Success is not necessarily just completing a project on the precise date you set or utilizing the exact course or direction you had planned. Real success is arriving together at the same spot at the same time. Like fighter planes with bombers in WWII, the object is to stay together, make group corrections, hit your objective simultaneously and plan your next steps together.

Frequently, we observe leaders who attempt to control a company by rewarding team members for always being "right on track." Those who are off track are evaluated as not doing a good job. This process rewards people who hide the elements of their work that are not on track and find "creative" ways to report that they are, even when they are not.

It would be much more effective to teach people how to listen for signals that indicate they are off track; how to effectively communicate their position; and finally how to make accurate, timely and appropriate course corrections. These people will begin to value their efforts to communicate course corrections and vital changes to others.

The real key is to assume that you and all members of your team will be off course most of the time. Like a pilot, who assumes he may be off course even when all of his instruments tell him that he is on course, the constant focus is on the value of minute corrections that are communicated to the entire flight crew and translated into physical changes that alter the plane's actual course. The critical need is to communicate with others to find out how your "off-course excursions" could be altered to keep in sync with where others are also slightly "off course." Emphasis on constant course correction will keep the entire effort going in the right direction if your staff openly and positively affirms exactly where they are with each other. Communication is imperative!

Off-course denial quickly becomes "the death of a thousand injuries."

Internalize It or It Won't Work

It's the new craze. Everyone who is anyone has a "Palm Pilot." You have, no doubt, felt the pressure to purchase one of those little hand-held wonders that can maintain a continuous wireless connection to the web, as well as contain every phone number and address that you have ever used in your lifetime. It's a real mind-altering exercise to imagine how much information can literally be at your fingertips. Why would memorizing important milestones and dates be useful to your leadership strategy?

Internalization is a vital part of commitment. When we write things down we assume that we don't, or won't have to remember them. If dates and times are absolutely critical path to our corporate success, why wouldn't we internalize them?

At our seminars we often ask participants if they play golf. If we get a strongly positive answer from a particular participant, we ask when they will be playing next? The most common answer is a specific day and, upon further questioning, we get a precise tee time right down to the minute. When we don't get golfers, we go for a person who is looking forward to a vacation. Where, exactly where, will they be going? How will they get there? Where will they be staying? When will they be leaving to return? Who will be going with them? How much will it cost? Frequently they have specific answers for every question.

Isn't it amazing that these important events are all committed to memory, yet we take notes in a meeting that those in attendance deem to be critical to the success of the program? Do we return quickly to our offices and fill in the details from other resources, then commit to memory the entire process? Why do we routinely memorize vacation details but relegate our work to files? Exactly what will you be doing two weeks from this very moment – assuming you're not on vacation or playing golf?

Encourage your team to memorize critical path elements of your overall operational plan – complete with dates. Memorizing milestones is a way to extend commitment to actually getting the job done. Emphasize that you are asking them to memorize specific events and dates so that they can report back if they feel they are a bit off track. You certainly don't want them to conclude that you don't want to hear that they aren't "getting the job done on time." Keep it positive. You might want to use birthdays, holidays or tee times for milestones to ensure that this procedure adds strength and fun to your corporate culture, not detract from it by making this a compulsive activity. Amazing as it may seem, we have never had attendees at a *No Feet In Concrete* seminar who were unable to memorize **all** of their critical path activities and dates.

Summing It Up

It turns out that leadership is really a process and not a series of steps from one obvious solution to the next. Success refreshes itself and often creates its own need for change. While some people fear this self-created change, strong leaders welcome it and maintain confidence that the process will bring new solutions to the table as needed.

It is this confidence in process that is the hallmark of a great leader. Solutions will often reside within your staff or in the entrepreneurial world itself. Commitment to process will help you avoid operational paralysis if you don't see the exact next stone in the path. If you listen carefully and look for the solutions hiding in the process itself, you will consistently move forward toward your next operational goal.

Focus can breed confidence and direction. Those who learn this secret profit from it for a lifetime. Continual distraction is the Achilles heel of strong leadership. Focus is essential and indicates your serious commitment to the success of both the entire enterprise and those important individuals who work to see it happen.

Next we discussed the problem of pushing on rocks. Many times the more we discuss problems, the more strength we assign to them. Continually discussing weaknesses and threats builds them up and stifles enthusiastic effort. Basically it's a bad habit that, when eliminated, will instantly add strength and focus to your work and the work of those around you.

By allowing staff members to present concepts to you only as strengths and opportunities, you will prevent them from putting their monkey on your back. It will also mean that you will get solutions attached to things that were previously presented as a problem. Leaders who continually find the monkey on their back often miss this valuable opportunity. By utilizing this concept in your strategy, you will develop the expectation that you are a leader and not their doer and decider when schedules get cramped. Remember how useful your **SOS** rubber stamp can be when dealing with moving monkeys. Team members who complain without solutions are the ultimate **SOS.**

You may want to stress the value of having your staff assume that they are continually off course, rather than only rewarding them when they say they are on course. The off course assumption is usually a more accurate reflection of operational reality and encourages communication and coordination of effort. The assumption that everyone will be off course in some small way produces far more useful feedback for everyone.

Finally, many leaders find it useful to encourage their team to memorize important dates and events. This process increases commitment to group effort. You should utilize this element if your group tends to lack the confidence that each team member will meet group expectations and goals. Remember, if you use this technique, be sure to make it fun. People may still want a Palm Pilot for the stuff that really isn't all that important. Toys do make people happy if you keep them in perspective.

Questions and Actions

1. Have you ever been afraid of the results of a successful enterprise? Did it cause you to falter a bit when you got started? Have you ever wanted to start your own company or write a book? What if it was *really* successful? How would it change your life? Has this fear of success held you back?

2. Where do you see people pushing on rocks? Make a list of issues that are continually discussed without possible solutions. Formulate the toughest issue into the form of an opportunity. What could you achieve if you were able to address the opportunity with a solid solution?

3. Ask someone you work with what issue you complain about most often. Turn it into an opportunity and follow the process to a powerful solution that can be presented to your team.

4. Do you have your SOS rubber stamp yet? Could you actually print it on someone's hand if they came in and complained after you explained that they were to always formulate opportunities and strengths?

5. The next time you are driving, take note of how long you can drive, with cruise control on, without changing the steering wheel in any way. Sure you can use the horn, but we are not liable for the results of this process if you end up bending fenders!

CHAPTER 6

The Frame:
Seven Leadership Essentials

"We struggled for years to try to get our company to react to the market. The opportunity was passing us by and our former President just didn't have the skills to get us to move forward. He certainly knew the industry, and he genuinely wanted to make it happen, but he just didn't see how to get us to commit to making that all-important first step together. He lacked a clear focus and kept recycling the same ideas he had used for years.

"Our new President saw the big picture, listened to what we were ready to do, focused our department heads on true leadership skills and inspired us, and big things began to happen. What a difference!"

- Leaders

- Seven Elements of Leadership – In Order!

- A Curious Reverse Order

- Integrity at All Times

Leaders

We all intuitively recognize great leaders. They exude a strong sense of purpose and a relentless commitment to success. Brilliant leaders move people together to take advantage of an opportunity and turn it into a profitable achievement. They bring out the best in their staff and ensure that those they lead have the opportunity to become leaders as well.

We determined in previous chapters that great leaders don't just bark orders, yell, scream and threat or try to establish consensus. They don't simply set up goals and objectives, and they certainly take more than "one minute" to do what they need to do.

We also know that the job of an entrepreneurial leader in this radically changing world requires that they create new leadership styles for each new opportunity. *No Feet In Concrete!* Everyone enjoys being around leaders to be a part of a big picture and the process of creating success.

What are the qualities of great leaders that allow them to attack opportunities in this unique manner? What is it about them that continually brings out the best in the people they lead? Are these special qualities something that leaders are born with or something they learn? How do they put themselves into positions to be recognized as leaders? How do they place themselves in situations that take advantage of their unique skill set? We recognize strong leaders, but do we know what makes them unique?

Seven Elements of Leadership – In Order!

While observing powerful leadership, seven steps were

identified that leaders seem to display within their unique leadership styles. These seven vital signs are observed in nearly all powerful and effective leaders. Each critical element is addressed and builds upon the one before it, resulting in a powerful, functional leadership style.

Moving back down the chart to ineffectual leadership can be as quick and unnoticed as it is insidious and difficult to turn around. Indeed, these seven essential elements of leadership are built one upon the next, but they will just as predictably vanish, in reverse order, if they are not meticulously cultivated and constantly maintained.

1. Integrity

The beginning point for all effective leadership is integrity. It's not the kind of integrity that is often identified with "nice" behavior or simply telling the truth. Many of the world's most prominent and highly effective leaders have operated well beyond the maintenance of a gracious, truthful demeanor. The word that begins to reveal the ground of integrity is *reliability*. And although the word "reliability" is a good beginning spot, a more appropriate definition of integrity, in an entrepreneurial world, is *internal consistency*.

Internal consistency works when people do what they say they will do. This is the first step that leaders use to build their position and the trait that cultivates the confidence of those they lead. Note again, we don't just lead those who are below us on the old _____ chart. We lead people on the "leadership diagram." When we are recognized as leaders, we lead people who are all around us. Internal consistency is the ultimate beginning.

One of the best examples of this kind of integrity driving leadership was an early experience that I had with a salesperson who produced some amazing numbers.

A California-based company's Vice President of Sales and Marketing asked that I take a look at a direct sales organization to determine areas where there was room for improvement. True to most sales operations, there was a wide disparity between the most effective and the least effective salespeople. While the numbers certainly didn't lie, everyone had their opinion as to why this was the case. In preliminary discussions with various people in the company, a number of differences became evident. While there were some territorial and climatic variances, there was no way to easily account for the vast discrepancy in performance between the members of the sales staff.

I asked if it was possible to travel to a few territories to get some windshield time with some of the company's best performers. Within a week, I was face to face with the handpicked, top producer. To my surprise, as he greeted me in the airport, he displayed great difficulty speaking. I fought my own personal embarrassment, while he displayed very little. How could this man, with such a strong stutter, be a top sales producer for his company and lead so many customers to use his products?

After discussing his territory and some of the techniques that worked for him (one word at a time), I bluntly asked why he had chosen a career in sales and how had he so obviously triumphed in spite of difficulty speaking. His answer has stuck with me for years.

> "My stuttering has always reminded me to put my effort into listening. Obviously I try to talk as little as possible; people don't want to listen to you talk anyway. They don't give a damn how you talk as long as you listen to them and do whatever you agree you will do. People continue to give me business because I listen to what they need. They know that if I say I can do something, I'll do whatever is necessary to get it to them – it's just that simple."

Internal consistency – doing what you say you will do – is the basis for all leadership. As you develop your plan, this habit will serve you well. Working within integrity communicates that you expect everyone to live by this same simple principle. As integrity becomes a fundamental element in your process, every aspect of your plan will be taken more seriously. As you act consistently upon the tasks that you have agreed to do, those you lead will do the same.

People around you make integrity judgements every day, and internal consistency is as important as any single act when you establish yourself as a viable leader. This is the perfect example of the old saying that "you can't break the rules, but you can break yourself against them!" Even bending the rules to make things happen "just once – in this situation" will immediately destroy your ability to effectively lead anyone.

2. Focus

When you establish that you are able to deliver integrity on a consistent basis, you are ready to bring focus to your big picture. Everything you do must continually shine light on the same image and purpose. If one of your staff members overhears you explain the big picture to someone else, they should hear precisely the same narrative you initially gave to them.

The same comment is even more cogent in the communication of your Jugular Issue. The entire purpose of maintaining a Jugular Issue is to establish that final focus on the outer edges of decision making. The consistent communication of your Jugular Issue and the application of it to your own work will, in and of itself, create even more intense focus.

Focus is viral. When you display a single focus upon (1) a successful outcome, (2) a skillfully crafted process and (3) a timely Jugular Issue, it will reliably infect others. Success within a complex entrepreneurial world is always the result of constant focus.

Unfortunately, distraction is just as viral. It inevitably spreads to others with constant disruption and removes speed, efficiency and personal satisfaction. The streets of failure are paved with distraction. Distraction always confuses people and incessantly detracts from effective leadership.

3. *No Feet in Concrete*

Once you establish your personal integrity and display a clear focus upon your objective and its ongoing process, the big picture and your Jugular Issue, it's time to get everyone's feet out of concrete. Discussions of the old ways of doing things won't qualify you as a leader in an entrepreneurial world.

You should give special attention to letting go of those drivers that you have identified as SOS. Each person has their own set ways of doing things. They find comfort in doing things in the same old way, time and again. Get out your SOS stamp and have at it. You'll recognize SOS in comments that begin with these kinds of negative statements:

♦ But we tried that before . . .

♦ But we've always done it that way . . .

♦ Based on my/our experience I don't think . . .

♦ I just know that it won't work because . . .

When you see genuine SOS grab the reins of movement, refocus your group on the opportunity before you. You will need to affirm to your staff members that they are most useful when they find fresh new ways to do things. Your confidence in their ability to seek new solutions is a powerful motivator.

You don't want to confuse experience with SOS. Experience can be a great teacher unless there has been a significant change in some element of what you attempt to do or the resources that you currently have to get it done. In a chaotic entrepreneurial world, since change is more likely than static state, you can be sure that it's worth a solid look before you allow experience to dictate process.

A few years ago, one of our top videographers came into my office to discuss a specific problem that had plagued our production department for months. Being somewhat frustrated by the problem myself, I asked him what he thought we should do to put the problem to bed forever. After a moment, he suggested essentially the same solution he had offered months before. I began to feel the monkey on the back of my chair, heading directly for my neck. I reached for a pencil and wrote on a piece of paper the following words, and slid it across the desk.

Your feet are in concrete!

After a thoughtful pause, he picked up the pen with a smile and wrote, "It isn't 'set' yet!"

We both saw the need for a dramatic, new solution to the problem, or we would be back at it in a couple of months, discussing the same fundamentals. Indeed, he soon found a solid, new opportunity hiding in the problem, and I immediately recognized the phrase that would become the foundation of our search for a dynamic leadership style for our growing company, our leadership seminars and now this book.

No Feet In Concrete!

If you turn your daily focus away from doing the SOS, you certainly will be recognized as a dynamic leader. As we mentioned earlier, simply executing a plan is far different from leading people around you to a completely new and more effective position.

Beyond discovering opportunities, one sure sign of a leader is the ability to reveal innovative ways to get things done while encouraging others to seek fresh process as well. Getting your feet out of concrete becomes the basis of new thinking.

4. Revealing New Paradigms

As soon as those around you perceive that your feet are *not* in concrete, they will look for you to reveal more effective and satisfying ways to accomplish common purpose. Without these tools, you will only be seen as throwing your staff into a chaotic world of opportunities with the SOS process, rather than actually freeing them up to do dramatically better work.

As mentioned in an earlier chapter, looking for new methods is a continual process of discovery. Your confidence in finding and revealing brilliant solutions will fuel the process.

> A commonly held explanation for the success of the Chicago Bulls was the contribution of Michael Jordan. No doubt Jordan was, at least, one of the finest to ever play the game. No doubt that other players on the team will find their way to the Basketball Hall of Fame.

> No doubt, as well, that the Los Angeles Lakers of the late 1990s were in a slump. No shortage of talent there . . . good players cycled in and out of the team. The team owners finally had to admit that, while the Lakers were capable of playing great basketball, they couldn't put it together to win a championship. Shaquille O'Neal, another one of basketball's greatest, couldn't seem to achieve a championship with any team.

When the team that made up the legendary Chicago Bulls began to break up, it became evident that Phil Jackson was no longer interested in coaching the team. Likewise, the current players knew that they would find it difficult to succeed without Jackson.

The Lakers' management knew that Jackson was exactly who they needed. They had a group of headstrong individuals playing a team sport. Jackson was the consummate team-building coach, able to see unique potential and link good players into a championship team. The question was, could Jackson produce a championship team in Los Angeles without Jordan, Pippin and the other players that made miracles happen year after year in Chicago?

The answer was that Phil Jackson didn't go to Los Angeles and do the SOS. He had a totally different set of star players in different positions, each with radically different skills. The Bulls had been the most confident team in basketball, while the Lakers exhibited very little confidence in their ability to win a championship. Many sports writers openly suggested that Jackson was making the biggest (and perhaps the first) mistake of his career by accepting a position to coach the Lakers.

At the end of Jackson's first season coaching the Lakers, which culminated in their first championship in 12 years, it became clear that Jackson never did try to make the Y2K Lakers look like the Bulls of the past. In his very first season he discovered what was hiding in the Lakers that would link them into performing like a first-place team and make a championship become a reality. As he began to carve away what was preventing them from winning, he revealed an entire new way for the team to play together, installing a completely new paradigm.

If Jackson had gone to Los Angeles with his feet in concrete he would have tried to utilize his old formula for Chicago's success and then set out to make the players look and act like the Bulls of the past. In reality, isn't this what we see managers (not leaders) attempt to do every day? Facing a new problem (not opportunity) they apply the same old ways of doing things. While trying to meet new objectives, their big effort is spent getting their staff to do the things that the old paradigms required.

A true leader knows that each new situation requires a totally new paradigm, even if (like the Lakers and the Bulls) you are attempting to reach the exact same goal. Great coaches are successful leaders because once the season begins they look for new ways to win with the strengths and opportunities that their team holds. Recruiting only happens once a year – coaching happens every day. Sadly, it is often the case that a coach will blame the loss of a game on the players. You can tell when coaches operate in this mode when they constantly talk about recruiting as a response to losing games.

When faced with a breakdown in a group endeavor, great leaders always focus more of their thoughts on how they could have lead the process in a more successful manner, even resting the primary blame for the failure of a staff member on themselves. Effective leaders take personal responsibility for the entire venture and the success of every player. Not that they take credit for the contribution and work of others, but leaders do accept the responsibility to discover the *right* new paradigms and hold themselves accountable for the success of the overall process.

5. Linking

Leaders are linkers. How often have we heard the old saw, "one weak link will break the chain?" Conversely, we often see people in leadership positions fall far short of success because they fail to link every member of their team. This is the essential next step in the leadership process.

When you have discovered the new paradigm that has been carved from the opportunity at hand, every member of your team must feel that they have made a vital contribution to the total process. If this is not happening, you need to make some quick course corrections to ensure that the team you have assembled is *exactly* what and who you need to get the job done. Don't try to move to the next step until you get this one solved.

It is amazing how often managers look aside, avoiding the single element that will dependably destroy the entire function of their chain in every case. Once they make the mistake of recruiting the wrong people or feel stuck with a team they have been given (especially those who make a point of destroying team activity and effort), they hang on to those weak links until they have put a crippling grip on the entire situation. It only takes one person on a team to destroy the power of real teamwork. This is a condition that deserves to feel the edge of the blade. All too often, managers hold on to a person because they fear what would happen if they didn't have them in the slot they fill. It is better to have no one at all in a position than to have a boat anchor that merely fills a seat. The display of any commitment to a boat anchor will destroy your ability to lead the competent players who want to drive to total success.

Linking means that a leader, in every case, applies conscious effort to link *every* member of their team. Leaders may become frustrated with the performance of specific team members, but should in no case create a wedge between the people they attempt to lead. Weak managers often create distance between their team members as a tool to manipulate and control those people below them on the old _____ chart.

"Divide and conquer" is a means of defeating the opposition, but just as surely will apply failure to your own organization. As a leader (not a manager) your job is to link your entire staff into one powerful unit. Making this happen requires constant vigilance for any sign of people who make a habit of driving wedges. Regardless of their position, when the people you lead feel you are linking them and every other member of the team toward one single-minded process, they will identify you as a leader, regardless of your position.

Leaders are always linkers.

6. Commitment

Commitment always shows up on the lists of traits that leaders display. However, if you begin to display total commitment before you have established integrity, displayed focus, removed your feet from concrete, created a new paradigm and meticulously linked every element of your team, you will establish yourself as a leader on a foundation of sand. Others will quickly sense this to be overconfidence acting as a compensation device for an obvious weakness or simple naiveté.

If, on the other hand, you move along the list of leadership qualities and develop a well-linked group, then you will show your total commitment to helping them succeed. When you display total commitment to a well-grounded process that is linked to an opportunity of significant proportions, your commitment will engender commitment in others.

Many historic moments are remembered because the commitment, displayed by a few, led to a greater good for the many.

In the 1960s, President John F. Kennedy was faced with the temporary cold war technological victory of the Russians with the launching of the first earth orbital satellite, Sputnik. President Kennedy, with little scientific or technical input, challenged the United States scientific community to commit to "put a man on the moon and return him safely to earth before the end of the decade."

To land a man on the moon and return him safely to the earth required massive commitment, as the United States missile program had displayed one failure after another causing total disillusionment within the Congress and the public. While many saw it as completely impossible, some thought it was feasible but not before the end of the decade. Still others thought it to be both risky and useless.

Initially, a single person publicly committed to making the moon trip happen, and lead the United States' commitment to Science as a national priority. The National Aeronautics and

Space Administration (NASA) caught the spirit. In funding the process, the federal government saw the opportunity and adopted the commitment to make the nearly impossible a reality. People put their entire careers and lives on the line.

Several historians have reported that this effort was one of the most effective, focused and far-reaching peacetime endeavors in U.S. history. Scholars who have studied management and leadership have focused a good deal of attention on this spectacular success and the commitment it took to do it. In this case, President Kennedy's initial commitment to space exploration sparked the dedication of enough other people to reach the moon and return to earth safely before the end of the decade.

When asked about the popularity of President Kennedy, despite the ongoing controversy that surrounded his administration, many Americans respond that it was his sincere, public commitment to big issues that won the hearts of people around the world.

President Kennedy had a favorite story about commitment that he liked to tell because it revealed one of his finest characteristics, and his family link to Ireland.

In Ireland, tall, imposing stone walls often separated large estates. The walls seemed all the more arresting because you could not see what was on the other side. They could hide armed guards, dogs or other dangers. A fall would likely result in serious injury. When a group of Irish boys encountered a seemingly insurmountable stone wall that stopped them along their journey, they would all throw their hats over the wall as a statement of total commitment to move beyond the barrier.

Kennedy's staff members reported that when he expected total commitment from his staff, he would state that it was time for "everyone to get up and throw your hats over the wall." Kennedy understood the viral power of commitment and just when to use it to motivate his staff.

It is impossible to create leadership without personally displaying total commitment to all elements of your plan. You must publicly commit to applying every single facet of your unique leadership style to yourself in order to expect the total commitment of others.

Military leaders fundamentally understand the special power and role of commitment. A lack of commitment to any element of military strategy will infect itself into surrounding units. While this is especially true in combat situations, it also holds in all other facets of military life. When racism was tolerated at the top levels of military leadership, it was tolerated throughout the entire corps. When the top levels of leadership decided to commit themselves, they initialized movement toward the elimination of racism long before many other institutions even thought it to be a relevant problem.

Commitment, too, is completely viral. Beginning with one person, it can drive your team to success or inspire the world.

7. Inspiration

Inspiration – the ultimate test. This key factor serves as the final assessment you can use to determine if you are actually achieving elements one through six.

> **Integrity**
>
> **Focus**
>
> **No Feet In Concrete**
>
> **New Paradigms**
>
> **Linking**
>
> **Commitment**
>
> *And finally* . . . **Inspiration**

Each day you set out to lead others, you either inspire them and act as a full on leader, or you fall somewhere short and fail to fulfill your obligation and charge. It really is that simple.

If you inspire those you attempt to lead, it will be obvious to you and to others. They will want to be with you and work on the projects that you are responsible for completing. They will want to play for your team or find some way to transfer to your unit. They will want to join your political party or transfer to your school. People will want to be around you because you inspire their best work and create success. You know what they want to accomplish both professionally and personally. You know where to use their talent and how to value their contribution. Why wouldn't they see you as a leader and reach for your big picture as well? No rocket science here either.

If you inspire those around you, they will see you as a leader. If not . . . I'll save the ink, you know the rest of this paragraph.

A Curious Reverse Order

A curious reverse order happens when we lose our commitment to inspiring others at all times. Sure, there are days and times that make it tough to fulfill your full-time obligation to create and maintain your unique style of leadership. While you know that you will be recognized as a leader if you maintain the above flawlessly, it is far easier said than actually done on a continual, day-to-day basis. So what happens?

On that single day when you are not as (7) *inspirational* as you should be, your staff will likely forgive you by saying that you really weren't "up to your best today," but they will all still feel your total commitment to the program – "you'll have a better day tomorrow." With today's GenXers, your commitment will drive the process for a brief period of time. They will expect an inspiring, total leader tomorrow, or you will hear about it directly.

Integrity

Focus

No Feet In Concrete

New Paradigms

Linking

Commitment

If you rely too long on your commitment to drive the overall process, your staff will lose their focused drive, energy and creativity. Lacking this critical element of staff support, you will likely begin to slip backward farther down the list, eroding your perceived (6) *commitment* to the final success of your big picture goal. In this case, you will be forced to rely on your solidly linked staff (and *their* inspiration and commitment) to get the work done . . . not a strong position for a long-term leader.

Integrity

Focus

No Feet In Concrete

New Paradigms

Linking

If you don't perceive the destructive nature of the process at this point, it will surely wear away at your (5) well-*linked* staff. Sensing your weakness, they will look for leadership elsewhere. A strong group of people, looking for leadership and not finding it, will soon find reasons to violate the very chain that has held them together. Unfortunately, the dependence on a linked staff without your inspiration and commitment will, in and of itself, corrode the unity of your staff.

> **Integrity**
>
> **Focus**
>
> **No Feet In Concrete**
>
> **New Paradigms**

If you allow your staff to eat away at each other, you will certainly have limited success in installing (4) *new paradigms*. They will not have the confidence that your new process will work, nor will they have your total commitment to make it happen when they are challenged.

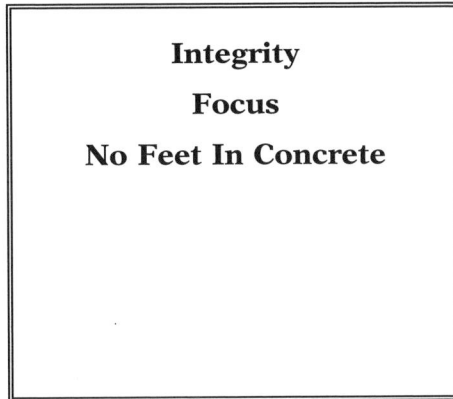

```
Integrity

Focus

No Feet In Concrete
```

When you stop revealing and utilizing new paradigms, you no longer have (3) *No Feet In Concrete* (and unfortunately your staff will likely follow you to the soft cement forms).

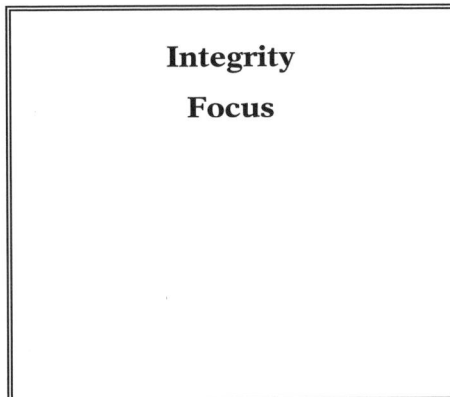

```
Integrity

Focus
```

It only requires a short period of time with your feet in concrete before you will be merely tolerated as a manager of old plans and a leader of none. As the cement begins to harden, you will lose your (2) *focus* on the big picture and your ability to even execute a plan. Distraction becomes the rule, rather than the exception.

Integrity

With your feet in concrete and no focus, no big picture or new paradigms, an unlinked staff eating away at itself, lacking commitment and having lost your daily obligation to provide inspiration, your only tactic may be to compromise (1) *integrity*. Without this first and final driver, you have left those you attempted to lead in an ever-changing, fast-driving entrepreneurial world without internally consistent direction or leadership . . . a sure sign of impending failure.

Integrity at All Times

One final word about integrity. Internal consistency is required at all levels and at all times. Unfortunately, any single slip within this category will ensure doom for your entire process. Any inconsistency here will incontestably destroy your ability to lead in minutes. And, most unfortunately, you become the poster child for not doing what you say . . . hardly a trait that will inspire trust and internalized accountability. While this sounds sensible, it is amazing how many leaders miss this critical principle of effective leadership.

The inviolate rules of internal consistency are simple. The principle to remember is that it's not OK for you to break the standards that you have set for others. You'll never be able to successfully break the fundamental principles you establish for your operation – you'll only break yourself against them.

Finally, if you meticulously maintain your activity within this test of integrity at all times, it will serve as a hallmark for you and your organization. Integrity is a constant source of both internal and external strength, providing critical energy in those pressure point moments when you need it most.

Summing It Up

There are seven imperative elements of effective leadership that form a frame for the construction of our unique leadership style.

```
Integrity

Focus

No Feet In Concrete

New Paradigms

Linking

Commitment

Inspiration
```

Beginning with integrity, we build leadership styles that continue through the process until we provide inspiration daily. This is no small task, but it is a dependable process that will ensure that we function as effective leaders for our unique opportunities, even within the exponential changes that drive the 21st Century. Rich, satisfying opportunities are abundant but often hide within our entrepreneurial world. However, without timely, dynamic leadership, all many people see is apparent chaos.

True leadership sees into the ivory. Insightful leadership carves unique opportunity and potential. Focused leadership creates big pictures with clarity and purpose. As you link your organization into one unity, your committed leadership creates inspiration and ensures success.

Inspiration is the test. If you can conclude that the people around you find you inspirational – you are right on target. If not, find where you are successfully operating on the list and get to work on the next level up.

Questions and Actions

1. Who has functioned as a real leader for you? Overlay the list of seven leadership essentials that have been identified. How did your leader address each of these categories?

> **Integrity**
>
> **Focus**
>
> **No Feet In Concrete**
>
> **New Paradigms**
>
> **Linking**
>
> **Commitment**
>
> **Inspiration**

2. Can you identify a time when someone you considered to be a strong leader slipped on the integrity issue? How did their internal inconsistency affect their ability to provide leadership for you? How long did it take them to reestablish your confidence?

3. Take a look backward. Where have you inspired others? It is likely that you were performing well as a leader at that point. We're ready to bet that you also had the other six essentials operating successfully.

4. It's your call, where do you want to function as a leader? At work, at home, in volunteer organizations? The *No Feet In Concrete* process allows you to create a leadership style that will work anywhere.

5. Create a list of the people you would like to lead, and put it on your mirror. Start to develop your own process right now – what opportunities are hiding here?

CHAPTER 7
Inspiration: The Catalyst

"When I think about people who have been important leaders for our company, they haven't always been the ones at the top. They have been those who have inspired us to make the very best products and deliver them with outrageous customer service. I can remember a salesperson who could get us to do anything and then convince the customer that it was just what we always did for our customers. Here's a situation where one of our salespeople actually led our whole company."

- Inspiration

- A Unique Contribution

- Moving Minds to Action

- Process Makes Perfect

- Inspiration In Everything

- Cause and Effect

Inspiration

Catalyst: the element that brings all factors together to allow an action to happen. Inspiration is clearly the final catalyst for successful leadership and achievement.

Some people are inspired by being near the ocean. Some are inspired by trees. Some people have been inspired by hearing a Bach chaconne for the first time, played by the young violinist, Hilary Hahn. Still others can find one simple Zen koan that will create internal motivation and profitable activity for years.

Inspiration is not a warm, fuzzy feeling that only makes us feel good for a few minutes. Inspiration is certainly not just a pleasant sensation that leads to nothing. Inspiration is an experience that provides energy that changes the way we respond to opportunity. Inspiration is an internal experience that changes our external behavior. If, for example, we are truly inspired by an experience in nature, it will forever change the way we approach the natural environment. True inspiration never stops at an emotional level, but resides as a catalyst in authentic changes of action.

If you want to control your sheep or cow, put it in a large green pasture!

Did you find this concept inspiring? Will it change the way you approach the people you want to lead? If it creates a change in the way you work with your staff, it has inspired you. No need for goals and objectives. No tests required. No reason for a performance review. If it worked, it will have been a catalyst for new success. Let's try it again.

There are four kinds of people in this world and each one dictates a different response:

> *(1) If a person doesn't know and knows that they don't know – educate them!*

> *(2) If a person knows but doesn't know that they know – wake them up!*

> *(3) If a person thinks that they know but doesn't know – shun them, they are fools. They prevent themselves from ever knowing!*

> *(4) If a person knows and knows that they know – follow them!*

Did you find that inspirational? Do you have members of your team who prevent themselves from ever "knowing" because they think they already understand – but don't? How about the other categories? Does the above give you insight that will actually change the way you respond to these different types of people? If it actually changes your activity, then it has inspired you. How about one more?

We act like leaders.

We are recognized as leaders.

We are accepted as leaders.

We are rewarded as leaders!

How did you respond to that? You now have the tools to create a powerful leadership style that will work for you. There are always people around you who would profit from your effective leadership (and leadership isn't small-particle physics). You know that if you create a unique leadership style, you will be recognized and accepted as a leader. Did the word "rewarded" stir up some commitment to putting the names on your mirror of the people who would appreciate your effort and respond to you and your leadership?

While some things provide inspiration to some people and other experiences inspire others, *great leadership inspires everyone!*

The key to inspirational leadership is that it is carefully linked to our priorities and goals and provides a path to our success. If it is tightly connected to our priorities, it immediately gets our attention. Inspirational leadership releases our energy to reach our goals, not because we have been managed, motivated, micro-manipulated or "smooth talked" into a slot that needs filled, but because it frees the true potential hiding inside.

A Unique Contribution

As you create inspiration around you, it is vitally important that you commit to creating your own style that fits the people you lead. If the style you create fits *you*, the people around you will see integrity in everything you do.

> *No Feet In Concrete* creates the "suit" that began with your measurements, instead of a generic "suit" that is altered to fit you. The results are obvious. The "suit" perfectly fits every unique aspect of your physique because it is tailor-made.

Moving Minds to Action

Inspiration changes behavior by revealing something that helps us see final success more clearly. Inspirational leaders provide the same function – they impart insight that brings out our best actions. It is this intensely personal and contemporary element that provides inspiration.

- ◆ We feel inspiration at the moment someone looks at our potential, commits to helping us carve away what isn't "seal", removes barriers and stands by to ensure our success. It incites courage to move forward and actualize our potential.

- ◆ We feel inspiration when a salient concept provides a clear direction to find our way through what seems to be useless confusion and chaos. It stirs our motivation to take the first step.

- ◆ We feel inspiration when that quiet voice speaks to us in an occasion of experience and draws us forward toward a more effective occasion.

- ◆ We feel inspiration when, in a moment, a co-worker becomes a leader for us and does something specific that makes it possible for us to realize a dream.

- ◆ We feel inspired to create more effective results when someone appreciates our work instead of just sending us a check each month.

- ◆ We feel inspiration when we see the first functional step beyond the barrier of conventional wisdom and leap forward to respond to a new opportunity.

In short, it is precisely inspiration that makes dreams become reality. Inspiration is your daily commitment to both your staff and to yourself – in every activity that you initiate. The more effective your leadership skills become the more easily you will inject inspiration into everything you do. As you become accepted as a leader, you will be expected to make inspiration happen every day. Inspiration moves minds to new action.

Today, many people, in the broadest range of endeavors, are inspired by the latest generation of leaders who provide a new wave of highly effective leadership in all corners of the world.

We refer to this new breed of powerful drivers as "Super GenXers." Motivated, focused and as ambitious as they are willing to put in "half days" (they'll let you to pick any twelve hours) seven in a row, these people will challenge every premise that you have ever assumed to be at the heart of good leadership. They demand inspirational leadership daily and gladly provide the same in return. In many ways, this book was inspired by those Super GenXers who have provided new leadership for our company. They have brought with them the most powerfully focused energy and leadership skills that we have observed in the history of our marketing communications company.

They will rattle your brains and demand your best, but you'll love every minute – they live to make the impossible happen every day.

Process Makes Perfect

It is impossible to simply walk into work one day and become a source of inspiration for those you lead. However, following solid process will reliably generate inspiration in every case. No clear process – no inspiration. With good process – inspiration happens.

Good process will generate a totally contemporaneous leadership model – responsive and fluid. When we think about great leaders, they are definitely a confluence of opportunity, need and skill that could only happen in that particular moment of time. Great leaders throughout history have known the secret of inspiration. Many times they moved ahead without any pure assurance of success. Their confidence was in right process, not seeing a clearly defined daily map to successful outcomes.

> *Follow the right process, and it will generate inspiration, which will drive right process.*

Imagine a great leader: Thomas Jefferson, Mahatma Gandhi, Winston Churchill, Franklin D. Roosevelt, Mother Teresa, a high school physics teacher or band director, a friend or coworker, your own parents or a civic leader who has inspired you – personally. Why were they so successful and why did you pick that particular person? They faced insurmountable odds. They addressed the nearly impossible. They committed to the process, not a singular solution. They carefully chose their Jugular Issue. For Gandhi it was the use of non-violence in India's defiance of the British Crown. For Roosevelt it was overcoming fear itself! Their total commitment to perfectly crafted leadership continues to create inspiration for people around the world.

These leaders did it all. Their process included the unique application of every element of leadership essentials in circumstances that could have easily forced them to succumb to what seemed like chaos. They each had different opportunities and drivers – different times and circumstances – with widely varying results. But, they all provided every facet of great leadership from integrity to inspiration.

They each became the perfect catalyst for inspiration, pulling all the extant elements together. Instead of reaching backwards and pulling in old concepts or patterns, they seized every aspect of the moment and wove it into a perfectly crafted strategy for success.

Inspiration In Everything

By the time you have created a full on leadership style that works well, you will see inspiration take over every element of your endeavor. When you see this happen, it's time to take a week off and give yourself credit for reaching a real milestone.

During the past few years, as our seminars and this book have been developed, I have looked for the perfect example of how inspiration can take over an entire enterprise. It turned out that it was not nearly as simple as I had anticipated. One can easily mistake zealous activity for real inspiration. More often than not, entities that are initially formed to provide inspiration often become consumed with internal issues and survival, forgetting their charter.

The example of an enterprise that seems to have installed inspiration and experienced a viral infection in every element of its operation is a company that ostensibly makes tea, but has clearly accepted that they are actually driven to create inspiration.

Consider the following quotes directly from two different brands of tea boxes:

> *Twinings Green Tea is a fresh, all natural tea (camellia sinensis) containing no artificial colourings, flavourings or other ingredients. When made in the tradition of the Orient, brew Twinings Green Tea for only two minutes. The lightly golden tea will have a very smooth, mellow taste just as it has been served for over a thousand years. For a more western flavour, brew for three or more minutes until the tea is a deep gold colour.*

On another brand's box of tea the following text is surrounded by an original painting of a confident, peaceful woman sitting on a fire breathing dragon . . .

> *"Harmony is the inner cadence of contentment we feel when the melody of life is in tune. When somehow we're able to strike the right cord – to balance the expectations of our families and our responsibilities in the world on the one hand with our inner needs for spiritual growth and personal expression on the other. Usually, when the distractions of daily life deplete our energy, the first thing we eliminate is the thing we need the most: quiet, reflective time. Time to dream, time to think, time to contemplate what's working and what's*

*not, so that we can make change for the better . . .
Learn how to pause."*

Sarah Ban Breathnach, *Simple
Abundance*. A Daybook of
Comfort and Joy, 1996 Warner
Books, Inc. New York.

While we enjoy both teas, is there any question in your mind
as to which company is selling tea and which company has
been infected with inspiration? Why do we have thirteen
varieties of one brand of tea and only two of the other? Clearly,
our family was caught up in a process that went far beyond
freshness and traditional taste. Yes, our family does like tea,
but we enjoy reading every side of every box of Celestial
Seasonings Tea. We rarely, if ever, read the varietal description
on the others.

The viral infection of inspiration has migrated to our
breakfast table and follows some of us to the office in little tins
that were provided as part of a tour that we took of the Celestial
Seasonings plant. Without mentioning our intentions to
anyone, we decided to just show up for a factory tour and see
how far they had taken their mission. We left with a large sack
of new teas (as if we needed them) and an experience that
reinforced every thought that we had ever had about the role of
inspiration at Celestial Seasonings.

+ The original artwork that appears on their boxes was
  proudly exhibited on the walls.

+ The quotes on their boxes were displayed everywhere.

+ Mixing and bagging tea is an inherently messy process, yet
  everything was spotless.

♦ The guide could not have been more proud of her work or the teas they produced.

♦ The City of Boulder, Colorado promotes the tour of Celestial Seasonings as one of the best experiences in the area.

♦ In short, inspiration was everywhere and included in every product.

What is most interesting here is that inspiration has driven the process just as the process has created inspiration. You may think you cannot possibly provide daily inspiration that will find its way beyond your office. You may ask yourself how you can provide inspiration to your coworkers and customers when you produce valves, deliver clean uniforms each day or make a new software product. You can do it because it's not your product that supplies the inspiration – it's your people. Your customers' association with you and your staff, who live by inspiration daily, will instill a virus that will drive the process. This is the essence of powerful branding. It is happening every day in every kind of endeavor. And it is becoming the expected norm for the new generation of leaders who insist on an environment rich with inspiration at all times and will settle for nothing less.

If you start with integrity and expect nothing less than inspiration, you will, in fact, become a powerful, more effective leader regardless of your current position. You will earn and deserve attention, and you will make things happen! Those around you deserve leadership of the highest order – you owe it to them to provide inspiring leadership at all times.

Get to it! You know what you are doing.

- Help those around you get their feet out of concrete.

- Work in sync with their deepest personal and professional objectives.

- Let them know that you won't settle for consensus-ship.

- Never subject them to tired, old management styles.

- Carve assets and attack the opportunities with total commitment and real inspiration.

- With their support and input, build a leadership style that will ignite your operation and utilize every last skill that they are able and ready to supply.

Purpose creates great leaders . . .

Leaders inspire everyone around them . . .

You will create great things together!

Cause and Effect

We want to know how you put all of this to work for your enterprise. We look forward to your input as you begin to develop your own leadership style and achieve a new level of operational success from your efforts. If you have questions, suggestions or are willing to publish your success story in one of our eLetters, contact us through our website at:

www.nofeetinconcrete.com

Sharing your success will inspire others. We look forward to hearing from you.